THE GOD OF TIMING

By Paula White

D0167147

Editing services provided by Joshua Lease and Aegis Editing www.aegisediting.com.

ISBN: 978-0-9861339-2-3

Printed in the United States of America

Acknowledgements

First and foremost I want to thank God for His unwavering grace, love, and goodness in my life. It is truly Him that I live, move, and have my being.

I am eternally grateful for the love of my life, my husband, Jonathan Cain. Your love, support, dedication, understanding, and commitment to me and my life purpose are the wind beneath my wings. You are my gift from God in His "due season." I love you, baby!

Brad, you have always been my heart and joy. I am proud of the amazing man you are and thank God for bringing me Rachel and Asher through you. My heart could not be happier and more fulfilled as our family and legacy grows in love and blessing beyond what words could describe.

I also want to thank everyone on my team at Paula White Ministries. So many people work so hard to help the message of Christ go out, and often people only see my face. Yet they would see little of me and hear little as well if there wasn't such a great team of hard working, faithful people making it happen behind the scenes.

I'd also like to thank my editor, Joshua Lease, for helping to share more about this message of God's feasts as he did with Your Divine Appointment.

Finally, I want to thank every supporter of my ministry and everyone who has ever prayed for the work God is doing here. It wouldn't be possible without your support – thank you!

Contents

Chapter 1

Principles & Practice

You're a detective, an investigator. Your life is about discovery and learning, and your assignment is uncovering the secrets of the greatest mystery in the universe—our great God and Creator. Your guidebook on this great journey of discovery is the Bible, and in it are all the clues you need to discover the plan for your life that God has intended from the foundation of the world.

But your destiny doesn't end with discovering the secrets of God's plan for your life: you must then use what you learn to let Him change your life forever. James urges us to "be doers of the word, and not hearers only, deceiving yourselves" (James 1:22).

You may never have thought about it like this, but God has an MO. If you have ever watched a detective show or a mystery, you know that investigators study those they are pursuing to learn how they operate—their "method of operation." A good detective gets into the head of the person he or she is passionately pursuing.

God has an MO—a divine pattern, order, and arrangement of things that He has followed from the beginning—and His principles have never changed. The order or arrangement of the Kingdom of God—God's method of operation—is in all things, and it's our job to study Him and learn His way of doing things so that we may reflect His Kingdom in our lives.

It is not enough to just learn about God, His methods, and His ways; we must let them change us from the inside out.

This journey of discovery and change is like when you first meet the person you want to marry. In this sweet time of falling in love, you learn all about the other person—all of the mannerisms, behaviors, and principles of their personality. Uncovering each aspect of what makes this individual unique and extraordinary is a big part of the process of falling in love. You learn all the little things, because you're completely captivated and can't help but study this person whose life is meshing with yours.

Learning about this person knits you together, changes you. You become more like them. Not only do you find out how they think and find yourself finishing their sentences, how they act begins to impact how you behave, as well, and you find yourself taking on their mannerisms, reactions, and behaviors.

Learning about God through studying His principles is like that—learning and discovering the traits and mannerisms of our Love. We don't do it out of obligation, as though we were under the Law; we do it as a heartfelt response to the love affair with God that sweeps us up into salvation.

And as we become enmeshed with our Bridegroom, He changes us from within, and we take on His thoughts, ways, and mannerisms.

Now, imagine this for a moment. What good does it do to learn all about the person you love if you do not apply what you learn? Perhaps your future spouse enjoys lilies instead of roses. How does it show what you've learned if you never buy her lilies? Or maybe your love enjoys a slow cooked roast. What good does knowing he likes this meal do if you never cook it for dinner?

Christianity, I say in my book Don't Miss Your Moment, is not just about knowing—it's about being and doing. It is not enough to study God's patterns and principles through the Old

Testament feasts—our divine appointments— we must use what we learn in our lives as a result of the love He has placed in our hearts.

The feasts we read about in the Old Testament were God's way of letting His people get to know Him. They were His way of showing them His mannerisms, thoughts, principles, and methods. By participating in the feasts, they grew to know Him more intimately.

We are going to be uncovering God's ways and thoughts as we look at the feasts He gave His people, but we will all face the same challenge the Israelites did: will we let what we learn change who we are?

Doing God's Ways

Isaiah 55:9 says, "For as the heavens are higher than the earth, so are My ways higher than your ways, and My thoughts than your thoughts" (NKJV). But His ways and thoughts are not unknowable—we can learn them. This learning is the process of getting to know our Love.

But simply knowing His ways isn't enough. We must do His ways as well!

We connect with God through His Word, through prayer, through worship, and in spending time with Him. As we do so, we begin to learn how He does things. His way of doing things rules and reigns in His Kingdom; we must let them rule and reign in our lives.

The word "kingdom" is made up of two words you already know—"king" and "dominion." Within a king's dominion things are done his way. God's Kingdom is no different; it operates on His principles and follows His divinely established patterns.

When we make His ways first, our lives become aligned with

His plans and promises for us.

Jeremiah 29:11 is a very famous and often-quoted verse: "'For I know the plans I have for you,' declares the Lord, 'plans to prosper you and not to harm you, plans to give you hope and a future'" (NIV). But we rarely consider the context in which this statement was made. The Jewish people were in exile, having disobeyed God for so long that He eventually let them be conquered and led away into captivity.

They were there in captivity because they hadn't let God's ways become their ways.

In the midst of their captivity, however, God is telling them to trust Him and to return to His ways. God had had enough of Israel rejecting His principles and commands, and before they would experience His freedom, they had to walk through their captivity and begin putting Him and His ways first (and only).

On the other side of their captivity was a promise: ultimately they would experience His prosperous, hopeful future—if they would repent and return to His ways.

We who know Jesus have the Holy Spirit within us to teach us His ways and His Word is full of His principles and methods. He revealed Himself to Israel and instituted feasts and celebrations to teach His people about Him and help them remember what He'd done for them. Together, we will look at how God's Kingdom operates by learning about the significance of some of these biblical feasts and celebrations. And as we learn this background, we must always remember this: all of God's covenant promises and privileges are released and received by activating the Word of God in our lives. Isaiah 1:19 tells us, "If you are willing and obedient, you shall eat the good of the land."

The feasts are not just about behaviors and commemorative celebrations; they are about the principles of Heaven and a reflection of the ways of God's Kingdom. The yoke of Jesus is not a burden—the traditions and religions of men are. We embrace the biblical feasts to draw closer to God by spending time with Him.

The Principles in the Feasts

The feasts of Israel were living memorials to what God had done for His people. They were not only to remember these divine acts fondly, but God's people were also to reenact and participate in them over and over again. This reenactment served as a way of bringing what God had done for their ancestors into their present lives, keeping His favor and blessings fresh on their minds and letting them impact their lives throughout the year. God had them relive the experience—the sights, sounds, the smells, and tastes—of the events that had shaped their Hebraic heritage.

However, God was not only trying to help His people remember what He'd done for them; He was trying to etch His principles and ways upon them.

Many Christians respond with something like this when I begin to teach on the biblical feasts: "I don't celebrate these feasts because I'm not Jewish. Why do we need to know about this as believers?"

This might seem like a valid concern, but it simply shows that they do not understand the component of the Old Testament which functions as a shadow or pattern of the New Covenant we have under Christ. The writer of Hebrews says, "The old system under the law of Moses was only a shadow, a dim preview of the good things to come, not the good things themselves" (Hebrews 10:1 NLT). Paul writes, "So don't let anyone condemn you for what you eat or drink, or for not celebrating certain holy days or new-moon ceremonies or Sabbaths. For these rules are only shadows of the reality yet to come. And Christ himself is that reality" (Colossians 2:16-17 NLT).

The Old Testament was a preview of what Christ would fulfill on earth. But Jesus Himself said that He did not come to abolish the Law but to fulfill it: "Do not think that I have come to abolish the Law or the Prophets; I have not come to abolish them but to fulfill them. For truly I tell you, until heaven and earth disappear, not the smallest letter, not the least stroke of a pen, will by any means disappear from the Law until everything is accomplished" (Matthew 5:17-18 NIV).

God established His principles to be kept forever. And while we as Christians may not observe the feasts as the Hebrews do, it is vital that we don't abandon the principles of what is important to God, because nothing that God established and Jesus fulfilled will ever become worthless.

The point of studying the feasts is not to bind Christians to celebration, ceremonies and rituals of the law. Rather, it is to learn about our Love, Christ Jesus, from the principles God established for His people before the time of Christ. These principles were revealed hundreds of years before Jesus fulfilled the promises of Scripture. In Christ, we have an excellent relationship with God, better than we could ever have through observing feasts and celebrations. However, the feasts and celebrations give us insight into the mind and heart of God.

As you learn of God's ways, it is my hope that you will implement these principles in your daily lives. Then, having learned about our Bridegroom and His ways, live as though His Kingdom were on earth. As our hearts say,

"May your Kingdom come soon. May your will be done
on earth, as it is in heaven" (Matthew 6:10 NLT).

Chapter 2

What It Means
to Put God First

When we practice God's ways and make His presence our priority, we remove the limits of what God can do in our lives. When we make Him first in all things, we are embracing the love that He has first shown us. We return it as we put the principles of His Kingdom into practice in our lives.

We all lead very busy lives, and at times it can be a challenge to figure out how God wants us to live. A well-meaning man was recently explaining how he had reorganized his priorities. The man realized he hadn't been reserving enough time for God. This realization caused him rearrange his schedule. He determined to put God first, his family second, his business third, and his pastimes and hobbies last.

He seemed genuinely proud of himself for having created this arrangement, and I did have to acknowledge that he was on the right track. But instead of congratulating him, I knew I needed to get a concept through, and that general support wasn't going to be enough.

"What would you say," I asked, "if I told you there's no such thing as priorities—that you can only have one priority in life, not many?"

He was utterly perplexed; he'd expected me to praise him. Instead, I pressed on: "What if I told you that God has to be your first and only priority?"

He was so surprised by my reaction that he was having trouble coming up with the words. "What about my family?" he asked, managing to find his voice.

I shook my head. "God. First, foremost, alone."

I let that sink in for a moment, and just when he seemed like he was going to explode with questions, demands, and perhaps anger, I explained something critical to him. A something that you too need to grasp.

There can be no priority but God; He must be first. In ranking his priorities, the man had missed the key to truly putting God first.

Making God first isn't about giving Him precedence over the other things, like visiting Him first in the salad bar of life. He isn't the first stop before we move on to other things. If we wish to build a solid foundation for our lives, we must invite God to be first in each and every area of our lives.

God must be first in our spiritual lives, of course, but He must also be first in our family lives. He must also be first in our professional lives. He even needs to be first in our pastimes.

Instead of a list of competing priorities with God at the top, imagine it like this: your life—every love, interest, concern, and passion—must be surrounded and enveloped by God.

Picture your family, your profession, and your hobbies all fitting within a box. Now, surrounding it on all sides is God—first. Or imagine your life in this way: that God is at the center—the hub—of a wheel and every other part of your life, like spokes on a wheel, are depending on Him first.

God isn't the first on the list: He transcends the list.

Putting God first in all areas of life is the foundation for your success this year, and for the rest of your life.

Distracted by Worry

God does not find our modern-day distractions unique or unusual. In fact, Jesus knew what our lives were like when He preached the Sermon on the Mount. I challenge you to take a moment, get our your Bible and read Matthew 6:25-34. Jesus paints a picture for the reader that explains how much our Heavenly Father cares for us.

He wraps up by saying,

> *Therefore do not worry, saying, 'What shall we eat?' or 'What shall we drink?' or 'What shall we wear?' For after all these things the Gentiles seek. For your heavenly Father knows that you need all these things.* **But seek first the kingdom of God and His righteousness, and all these things shall be added to you.** *Therefore do not worry about tomorrow, for tomorrow will worry about its own things. Sufficient for the day is its own trouble.*
> *(Matthew 6:31-34 NKJV)*

You have no doubt read this before, and we can easily gloss over what Jesus is saying and assume we've heard all this before. Yes, Jesus is talking about worries, but it's more than that. In the King James Version, instead of "worry", it says we should "take no thought" for these concerns of life. In the original Hebrew, this translates as "don't be anxiously careful" about the temporary things of this life that Jesus is talking about—our clothes, our food, our homes.

Instead of being preoccupied with the things of this life, people of faith are to take a radically different track: we are to "take no thought" of them. Instead, we are to seek Him first and trust that He will take care of all these other things. Worry and anxiety will clutter your spirit and ultimately be fatal to your faith.

Now, let's read this same passage again, this time in the Message version. Just picture Jesus speaking directly to you as you read this:

> *What I'm trying to do here is to get you to relax, not to be so preoccupied with getting, so you can respond to God's giving. People who don't know God and the way he works fuss over these things, but you know both God and how he works. Steep your life in God-reality, God-initiative, God-provisions. Don't worry about missing out. You'll find all your everyday human concerns will be met. Give your entire attention to what God is doing right now, and don't get worked up about what may or may not happen tomorrow. God will help you deal with whatever hard things come up when the time comes.*

Instead of having God as one of many priorities, even when placed first, and then ranking the other concerns of life, we're to live very differently—giving our entire attention to what God is doing right now.

This requires an intimate understanding of how to make first things first—and knowing that we can have only one priority, and it must be God.

One of the greatest writers of modern Christianity, C.S. Lewis, summed up the problem of competing concerns like this: "Put first things first and we get second things thrown in: put second things first and we lose both first and second things." In his essay First and Second Things, he wrote, "You can't get second things by putting them first. You get second things only by putting first things first."

In my book Don't Miss Your Moment, Rabbi Daniel Lapin, founder of the American Alliance of Jews and Christians, shared "C.S. Lewis' statements are so liberating, because when you identify your priority, everything else falls into its proper perspective... There has to be one thing that's first. And then there's everything else."

In other words, seek first the kingdom of God and His righteousness, and all these things shall be added to you.

First Things First

God clearly tells us to seek Him first. The question we all have at one time or another is how we do this—how do we seek God? Believers have asked this for centuries, and God has provided answers for them, and for us.

Chief among the ways we seek God is through His Word, which will never fade or pass away. God told Joshua always to keep it on his lips and to meditate on it day and night. Seeking God through His Word came with a promise: "For then you will make your way prosperous, and then you will have good success" (Joshua 1:8 NKJV). Paul tells us hearing God's Word is how faith comes.

These are just a few of the promises of the Word, but it's obvious: the more we seek God through His Word, the stronger our faith becomes and the better our lives will be.

Along with the Word, we also seek God through prayer. Just as God told Joshua to keep the Word on his lips, Paul admonishes us to pray without ceasing. Prayer is, quite simply, talking to God, and the Word is likewise full of promises about the power of prayer. As we pray, we align our hearts with God through relationship. We learn about Him through His Word, but we get to know God intimately by spending time with Him in prayer and by setting time aside for Him.

This concept of setting times aside for God as holy is at the foundation of the biblical feasts and holy seasons.

Firstfruits

The practice of firstfruits was a reminder that all first things belong to God—a principle found all throughout the Word. David writes, "The earth is the Lord's, and everything in it, the world, and all who live in it" (Psalm 24:1 NIV). From the first day of the week to the first month of the year to the firstborn to the first portion of our income, the Lord established that all firsts belong to Him.

When you study firstfruits in the Word of God, it is imperative that you understand the principle behind firstfruits. Again, all firsts belong to God. He lays claim to them. It is the irrevocable giving over or back to God what already belongs to Him. It's important to clarify this because there is a firstfruits feast (or divine appointment), the tithe is a firstfruit, there is a firstfruit offering, and Christ is the firstfruit of the brethren. So that you can put Scripture in proper context, simply remember that all firsts belong to God. I could write volumes of books on this principle alone!

Before we look at the initial mention of this principle in Scripture right after the Garden of Eden, let's take a quick look at how God introduced it to the Israelites through Moses during the Exodus from Egypt:

> *After the Lord brings you into the land of the Canaanites and gives it to you, as he promised an oath to you and your ancestors, you are to give over to the Lord the first*

offspring of every womb. All the firstborn males of your
livestock belong to the Lord. Redeem with a lamb every
firstborn donkey, but if you do not redeem it, break its
neck. Redeem every firstborn among your sons.
(Exodus 13:11-13 NIV)

God was fulfilling a promise to His people by leading them into the Promised Land, but their (eventual) obedience by going in, and His blessing upon them, came hand-in-hand with the principle of giving Him the first and best as part of His covenant with His people. God declares that all first things belong to Him to establish a redeeming covenant with everything that comes after.

It seems counter-intuitive at first glance—sacrifice the first and best to God? Can you imagine trying to explain to your children why, when the family sheep gives birth to its firstborn male, that you sacrifice it to God?

It seems so wasteful—on the surface.

But God was establishing a principle for His People that if they gave the first to Him, He would bless the rest. And the blessing He'd bestow on everything that came after would more than makeup for the sacrifice of the firstborn. This is the nature of the principle of firstfruits.

The word "firstfruits" contains the connotation of a promise to come and shares the same root word, "bekhor," with the word "firstborn" in Hebrew. Think on that for a moment—the very word contains the hope of the promise to come.

So a Hebrew family, herders who rely on the strength and multiplication of their flock, are to kill the firstborn and offer it as a sacrifice back to God. But God, in the very language used to describe the principle, provides a promise to them for their obedience: give me the first, and I will bless the rest.

This principle is as alive and well as our God is. Although we don't practice with the same rituals as under the law, we are not released from the principle of firstfruits in the New Testament.

Principles of Firstfruits

Firstfruits contains principles we should learn that have to do with God's primacy and the promise He gives to us.

The first principle is that God lays claim to every first thing. Whether it's the first of our income, the first of our herds, or the first of our time, it belongs to God. Exodus 23:19 and 34:26 says, "Bring the best of the firstfruits of your soil to the house of the Lord your God" (NIV). (And any time the Bible repeats itself, it is not an oversight: it means we are to give even more attention to whatever God thinks is so important that He says it more than once.)

The second principle is that the first part spiritually represents the total or whole. The firstfruit sets the pattern or establishes the destiny that will govern the rest. Romans 11:16 tells us, "If the part of the dough offered as firstfruits is holy, then the whole batch is holy; if the root is holy, so are the branches" (NIV). In other words, if the first is holy (because the first is given as a sacrifice to God and therefore redeemed), then the whole thing is holy. The first sets the tone for the rest. This principle reaches back to the time of creation, where God established the principle that every seed reproduces after its kind. The first determines the destiny of the rest.

The third principle is the promise: giving God the first lets Him bless the rest. The wisest man to ever live, Solomon, penned these words: "Honor the Lord with your wealth and with the best part of everything you produce. Then he will fill your barns with grain, and your vats will overflow with good wine" (Proverbs 3:9-

10 NLT). As few of us have barns to fill with grain or vats that can overflow with wine, today we might say He will fill our lives with His blessings and prosper us, even as our souls prosper.

Later in the book, I want to show you how Jesus fulfills this principle of firstfruits and that He is, in fact, the ultimate Firstfruit. However, before we move on, I want you to linger just for a moment with this thought:

By obeying God's ways, you possess the ability to direct the destiny of each part of your life. You are not helpless, swept along by winds of fate. You have the keys, through the principle of firstfruits, that will let you receive the best from God.

So often, people think that God is trying to get something from them. They believe He's demanding, selfish, or petty, but nothing could be further from the truth. Because God isn't trying to get something from you...

...He's trying to get something to you. Would you like to know what?

Chapter 3

Devoted to God

Some people respond defensively after hearing about the principle of firstfruits because they feel God is trying to take something away from them. They act as though it's somehow wrong that God tells us to give the first part to Him.

"After all," they ask, "what does He need with sheep or our money? Why should He test us by making us give Him something He doesn't even need?"

To people who think this way, following God's principle of firstfruits seems like jumping through hoops to get blessings from a capricious, power-corrupted God.

It's no wonder they don't get it. Those who see God like this never will achieve understanding.

The very first thing I urge people to understand is that, while He doesn't need it, God knows we need to give to Him—it's for us, not for Him. You give to God out of love, honor, and obedience. You give to God out of covenant.

An underlying principle sits just beneath the surface of this policy of giving God the first and best that I want you to grasp. Without this, you cannot wrap your heart around the principle of firstfruits.

This world is under a curse. It has been since sin entered the world through Adam and Eve, who did not honor the principle of firstfruits. They did not give the first to God; they consumed it themselves. And it's had a cost to be paid every day since. Disobedience will bring some form of "destruction" into our lives.

The principle of firstfruits is so powerful that when Adam and Eve started creation on the wrong foot at the beginning, it cursed everything that came after. Paul writes,

> *Nevertheless death reigned from Adam to Moses, even over those who had not sinned according to the likeness of the transgression of Adam, who is a type of Him who was to come. But the free gift is not like the offense. For if by the one man's offense many died, much more the grace of God and the gift by the grace of the one Man, Jesus Christ, abounded to many.*
> *(Romans 5:14-15)*

Jesus set a new order. As the Firstborn and Firstfruit of God, He could establish a new relationship with humankind. In 1 Corinthians 15:23-24 we read,

> *But there is an order to this resurrection: Christ was raised as the first of the harvest; then all who belong to Christ will be raised when he comes back. After that the end will come, when he will turn the Kingdom over to God the Father, having destroyed every ruler and authority and power.*

To understand why we must give God the firstfruits, you must grasp this: God demands the first because it redeems the rest from the curse!

Giving God the first is a method of redemption where He

rebukes the curse for our sake. We will get into redemption more thoroughly later in the book, but it is vital that you understand that giving God the first has nothing to do with His needs and everything to do with meeting our needs through His grace and provision.

Rabbi Lapin writes that the principle of firstfruits "is what triggers the windows of heaven." We do not give God the firstfruits to appease a petty god; we do it to invite Him into our lives and to bless all that comes after, snatching it back from the corruption that is on it since original sin.

I see this often in the area of tithing, a part of firstfruits, which we'll cover shortly. People get confused because they think God (or the preacher) is just after their money. The reality is that God owns it all already, and He is not trying to get something from you but trying to get something to you—blessing!

The Antidote

God asks us to give the first to Him to set the tone of our hearts and to open His windows of blessing upon the rest so that it is not under the curse. Listen as Moses explains God's methods and principles to the Children of Israel in Deuteronomy 8:16-18:

> *He gave you manna to eat in the wilderness, something your ancestors had never known, to humble and test you so that in the end it might go well with you. You may say to yourself, 'My power and the strength of my hands have produced this wealth for me.' But remember the Lord your God, for it is he who gives you the ability to produce wealth, and so confirms his covenant, which he swore to your ancestors, as it is today. (NIV)*

Beyond redeeming it from the curse, God understands that if we think we've achieved or earned blessings ourselves, it will swell us with pride. And perhaps the single quickest way to losing God's blessings is to become prideful. James, quoting Proverbs, writes, "But he gives us more grace. That is why Scripture says: 'God opposes the proud but shows favor to the humble'" (James 4:6 NIV).

In giving God the first, it becomes devoted it to Him, frees it from the curse, and serves as an antidote to the pride that will put us at odds with God. We are to "trust in the Lord with all your heart, and lean not on your own understanding; in all your ways submit to him, and he will make your paths straight. Do not be wise in your own eyes; fear the Lord and shun evil" (Proverbs 3:5-7 NIV).

So why do we give Him the firstfruits? It belongs to Him already, but He asks for the first and the best portion back to redeem it from the curse, as an antidote to pride, as an act of obedience and trust, and so that He can bless the rest. It is not for His sake that He calls us to understand this firstfruits principle; it is for our benefit so that He can bless and prosper us as we honor God by devoting the first to Him. This principle comes down to a heart issue that honors God in your lifestyle. Is God first?

Tithing

Let's look at tithing in context with firstfruits, meaning that the first tenth belongs to God according to His Word. A few pages ago, I mentioned that some people push back against the idea of giving God the firstfruits. They incorrectly think God just wants something from them, when in fact, He wants to give something to us—His blessing. They forget that God owns it all and that He's just letting us borrow whatever we own temporarily. He wants to keep us from becoming prideful, thinking that we accomplished our blessings ourselves. We just read that God opposes the proud, and I don't think I'm alone when I say that I would rather have God supporting me than opposing me!

Now, let me state perfectly clearly that this is not a heaven/hell issue. Your eternal destination was settled when you received and accepted all that God has done for you through His Son Jesus Christ. When you believed in Him as your personal Lord and Savior, because of His finished work on the cross, you became born again and justified through faith. That is a work only Jesus could do and a gift you can receive freely. Jesus told us that He has come to give you life—and life more abundantly (see John 10:10)! When we honor and obey God through His commands (His authoritative divine prescription), then we live out the will of God with His promise and provisions. He has an abundant (which means superior in quality) life for you!

What we offer to God as a firstfruit establishes His redeeming, protecting hand on whatever follows. We cannot expect the multiple blessings of God to manifest in our lives if we are not living by the principles He's established. He always does His part, but we must ask ourselves if we are doing ours.

When we withhold the firstfruits from God, it is robbing Him. Read what's probably the single most quoted passage on tithing, which is a firstfruit, now that you have the background to understand why God wants us to give our firstfruits tithes (the first tenth of your gross income) and offerings:

> *'Return to me so I can return to you,' says God-of-the-Angel-Armies. 'You ask, "But how do we return?"*
> *Begin by being honest. Do honest people rob God?*
> *But you rob me day after day. You ask, "How have we robbed you?" The tithe and the offering—that's how!*

And now you're under a curse—the whole lot of you— because you're robbing me. Bring your full tithe to the Temple treasury so there will be ample provisions in my Temple. Test me in this and see if I don't open up heaven itself to you and pour out blessings beyond your wildest dreams.'
(Malachi 3:8-10 MSG)

The word "rob" means to cover or to defraud. God is a giver (see John 3:16), so when you withhold His tithe, you are putting a cover or lid on God. Doing so defrauds Him from being who He is—your provider.

Do you see it? God is not trying to get something out of us; He's trying to get us to participate in His ways so that He can bless us so that He may be glorified.

For over thirty years I have served God, faithfully giving to Him His tithe. Like the psalmist, I can say that I have never seen the righteous forsaken or His seed begging for bread (see Psalm 37:25). Tithing was the beginning of progressive revelation that God showed me with firstfruits. As I was obedient in honoring God in this, I began to see in His Word the difference between the tithe and a firstfruits offering.

I remember distinctly the first time God whispered to my heart, "Give it all." He was asking me to honor Him with a firstfruits offering. I am so grateful I obeyed. He has blessed my life and purpose on earth far beyond what I could have imagined. Let me share a few of those occasions with you.

He demonstrated this principle to me personally when I was launching Paula White Ministries. I felt like the Lord told me to give it all—all the money I had. I didn't understand then, but I felt like God whispered, "Firstfruits," to me

At the time, I didn't know this principle of firstfruits, and giving away what little I had while trying to launch a ministry seemed foolish! But God wanted me to put it all in His hands so He could bless the rest, and I decided to be obedient by writing what was, to me, a large check to my spiritual father—everything I had, in fact.

Now, God does not tell us all to give everything we have all the time, but that is what He was asking of me. He was establishing something in my heart so that I would learn obedience and not become prideful: this was His ministry, not mine! He was teaching me to live in faith and obedience.

God wanted to be intimately involved in blessing the ministry, my purpose, and my life, and by giving when He told me to, I allowed Him to open the windows of heaven. I had obligated myself to over a million dollar contract, but I had no money in the bank to start the television broadcast! People began giving money to meet the growing needs, and they were often people I didn't know and certainly hadn't asked for help. Not only did God meet every bit of the startup needs, but He also gave a multi-fold harvest on the gift I'd given.

That is the power of firstfruits!

God is so brilliant and full of grace—I have no room to boast, and I could never think I built this ministry. Only God could do what He has done With the way the ministry has grown, survived through tough times, and the reach God has given it, the enemy would love to have gotten in and made any of us think we did it by our own might and power. But instead, God positioned my heart to stay humble as He poured out on us from the windows of heaven.

It has been from that core place that I remind all who have had the incredible privilege to serve through this ministry that it is only the goodness and grace of God that continually brings us through to reach others for His glory.

He Remains Faithful

It's time to ask yourself a tough question: Have you let God's principles position your heart, not so that He can bless you but so that you will not grow prideful when He fulfills His end by pouring out blessings on your life? Don't misunderstand and think this is just about money, either. Money is our riches in this day and age—not flocks or barns full of grain—so I urge you to take a look at how you use your money and ask yourself if you are practicing God's principle of firstfruits with it. In other words, are you honoring God by putting Him first in everything, including your finances?

If it seems as though your riches are devoured, like you just can't get ahead, or even as though God seems to be opposing you, this is the first area to check. Have you let Him position your heart so He can bless you by rebuking and redeeming you from the curse? Now, don't get me wrong—God does not curse you. He sent His Son, Jesus, to liberate you from the curse. However, when we are disobedient to God and His Word, we open the door to invoice demonic spirits and bring forms of destruction into our lives.

God will always be faithful to do His part. But you must ask yourself if you are doing yours.

People who accept that the tithe is an application of the principle of firstfruits often ask me how it should be done. The word "tithe" means ten percent, and this is where giving back to God begins—with the first ten percent of your income. Remember, it is all His to begin with because He created it, so in truth, the tithe is returning to God ten percent. Being a giver allows God to administer the antidote to greed, selfishness, and pride, and returning to Him the first (and best) establishes His blessing on everything that comes after.

So if you want to implement this principle with your finances, begin by returning the tithe to God—the first ten percent. Malachi says that we are to give to the storehouse, which I believe is the local church where you are being fed. Bring it all, and do so at a set time. We get these New Testament principles on tithing partly from what Paul taught to the church in Corinth: "Now about the collection for the Lord's people: Do what I told the Galatian churches to do. On the first day of every week, each one of you should set aside a sum of money in keeping with your income, saving it up, so that when I come no collections will have to be made" (1 Corinthians 16:1-2 NIV).

I don't want this to be about the nuts and bolts of tithing. I want you to understand how it fits in the pattern of firstfruits that God established, and I want you to know the blessings God wants to give you as you implement these principles in your life. He is trying to open you, the windows of heaven and pour you out as a blessing. He will rebuke the devourer (the spirit of waister) for your sake, and He will redeem the curse as you give to Him the first and establish the destiny of the rest. Whatever you do with the first governs what happens to the rest.

It's Never Too Late

God has established His ways and methods throughout the Bible, and our obedience to bring to God all of our firstfruits are what allow Him to bless everything that comes after. But what, you may wonder, happens if you've messed this up and haven't given the first? What if you ate it, like Adam and Eve? Through their sin, they cursed all creation.

If you fear that's what you've done, you may be wondering, "Is the rest cursed, no matter what?"

I don't want you to read about the principle of firstfruits and feel condemned, because "there is now therefore no condemnation to those who are in Christ Jesus, who do not walk according to the flesh, but according to the Spirit" (Romans 8:1 NKJV). But if you've read all this and see your life may be suffering because you haven't kept this principle, you may be experiencing God's conviction—a distinct prompting to change your behavior, repent, and do it His way.

You may be wondering if there's hope. Well, I assure you, there's always hope. All isn't lost, even if you "ate" your firstfruits.

Earlier, I told you that Jesus did not come to abolish the law but to fulfill it. So for any who have fallen short, who didn't know to give of the firstfruits and instead ate it, and who feel that the devourer has been eating your lunch, this next chapter is for you.

And I want to let you in on a secret: The sentence above describes all of us. Every single one of us has fallen short. And God knew it.

In fact, it is why He sent His Son. You see, Jesus wasn't just the offering for atonement for our sins; He's the new Firstfruit. And because of Him, even you—even all of us—can experience God's blessing!

Chapter 4

Jesus Is the New Firstfruit

We have all heard the phrase, "What they don't know won't hurt them." But the truth is entirely different: what we don't know can destroy us. Hosea 4:6 declares, "My people are destroyed for lack of knowledge" (NKJV). Grace is not blissful ignorance of God's ways, principles, and plans; it's receiving God's grace and Jesus' finished work and moving from sinner to saint, from lost to found in Christ, and from prodigal to child of God. There is a balance to God's Word—grace and truth!

But God loves us too much to let us stay in our ignorance and sin, and just because we get saved does not mean that we continue in our sinful ways. Paul writes, "What shall we say then? Shall we continue in sin that grace may abound? Certainly not! How shall we who died to sin live any longer in it?" (Romans 6:1-2 NKJV)

This is true for more than just ceasing our sinful ways after we're saved; it's also why we should be motivated to learn God's ways and how His principles work—and then do them.

What we learn from God's Word will sustain us, provide for us, care for our families and loved ones, give us victory, direct and protect our dreams, set us free, bless us, and so much more! God guarantees us wonderful promises in His Word. But receiving all of this is our choice. We must choose whether we will obey or disobey.

Seems easy enough, doesn't it? Choose the good, not the bad. Well, it turns out it's harder than you think—but thank God, there's help.

Choose Wisely

In Deuteronomy 11:26-28, God lays it out for us: "Look, today I am giving you a choice between a blessing and a curse! You will be blessed if you obey the commands of the Lord your God that I am giving you today. But you will be cursed if you reject the commands of the Lord your God and turn away from him and worship gods you have not known before" (NLT).

All of God's many blessings are laid before us, but they are set out with consequences. Remember what we discussed earlier in the book—that everything on this earth is under a curse because of Adam and Eve's sin. Jesus came and redeemed us, defeating death, hell, and the grave. However, just because He won and secured our victory doesn't mean we automatically walk in it.

Salvation is all-inclusive. It provides everything you will ever need, spiritually, emotionally, mentally, relationally, financially— all provision, both here (earthly) and eternally. Many don't reject salvation, but they do neglect it. Your abundant life and victory starts by receiving Jesus Christ as your Lord and Savior (see Romans 10:9-10), which reconciles you to God and gives you a new covenant with Him. This reconciliation opens up possibilities for your life through the provision of Jesus Christ. Giving the first to God is one way that allows Him to rebuke that curse for our sake.

This is the same principle: obeying God allows Him to bless us; choosing the curse subjects us to everything God wants to redeem and save us from.

Deuteronomy 28:1-6 contains some revealing verses in the Bible because they are God spelling out how much He'd like to bless us. It says,

If you fully obey the Lord your God and carefully keep all his commands that I am giving you today, the Lord your God will set you high above all the nations of the world. You will experience all these blessings if you obey the Lord your God: Your towns and your fields will be blessed. Your children and your crops will be blessed. The offspring of your herds and flocks will be blessed. Your fruit baskets and breadboards will be blessed. Wherever you go and whatever you do, you will be blessed.

(NLT)

What a promise! Blessing after blessing after blessing! God is a good God! There are principles throughout God's Word, and these principles are key to your receiving and walking in the promise of His covenant blessings. In other words, as we are obedient to walk in His ways, we will walk in His promises and provision. God is not a man that He can lie (see Numbers 23:19).

The problem was that despite knowing the consequences and the potential blessings, Israel couldn't do it—they seemed unable to choose life.

All we have to do to receive God's blessings is to obey Him. So why is that so hard? Humans have been making the wrong choices since the very beginning—from Adam and Eve to Cain, to Noah's day, all the way through to the Children of Israel and beyond to today. Every promise of God is ours when we apply and stand on His Word, obeying His principles.

So how is that going for you? Are you following God in everything? It's a serious question to ask yourself. You can justify all you want, or you can think that because you are doing better than someone else, all should be okay. This is not to anyone else, though—it's about you, it's about God, and it's about His unchanging Word.

Obedience Is Key

We've already looked at how Adam and Eve failed to secure the destiny of the future by offering firstfruits that would bless humanity. All they had to do was obey, yet they literally ate their firstfruits—and they inherited the curse. And, unfortunately, they didn't manage to teach their children any better.

Almost everyone is familiar with the story of Cain and Abel, even non-Christians. We've heard that they both brought an offering to God, but He accepted Abel's sacrifice and rejected Cain's. We think we know the story pretty well.

Many believe that this is a story about preference, but in fact, it's a text about obedience. And all too often, we don't understand the most important part of this story—why. Why did God reject Cain's offering?

We read in Genesis 4:3-5,

> When it was time for the harvest, Cain presented some of his crops as a gift to the Lord. Abel also brought a gift—the best portions of the firstborn lambs from his flock. The Lord accepted Abel and his gift, but he did not accept Cain and his gift. This rejection infuriated Cain, and he looked dejected.
> (NLT, emphasis added)

They both brought a sacrifice, so why did God accept Abel's offering? Was it because God is a carnivore? No, God did not reject Cain's offering because He wasn't eating gluten; He rejected it because it was not the first and best.

In King James, the words translated "time for the harvest"

are translated "in the process of time." A more literal translation of the Hebrew is, "at the end of days." Something, a period, had ended, and now there was a first or a new beginning. It was the time for a firstfruits offering, but while Cain brought an offering, he didn't fully obey.

It's not always doing what is wrong that nullifies the provision of God—but not fully doing what's right.

God cautions Cain about the road he'd started on. "'Why are you so angry?' the Lord asked Cain. 'Why do you look so dejected? You will be accepted if you do what is right. But if you refuse to do what is right, then watch out! Sin is crouching at the door, eager to control you. But you must subdue it and be its master'" (Genesis 4:6-7 NLT).

So, wasn't it good that Cain brought any offering it all? Definitely. But it was only partial obedience, and with God, partial obedience is disobedience. He didn't fully do what is right. "Remember, it is sin to know what you ought to do and then not do it" (James 4:17 NLT).

We read more in Hebrews about the difference in the brothers' offerings. "By faith Abel brought God a better offering [literally "a much more full or complete" sacrifice] than Cain did. By faith he was commended as righteous, when God spoke well of his offerings. And by faith Abel still speaks, even though he is dead" (Hebrews 11:4 NIV, notation by the author). This passage tells us that Abel had faith that was voluntary, complete obedience and following God's principles would yield a good result. He looked into the future and could see that his sacrifice held a promise.

Abel made his firstfruits offering, and then he obtained the Lord's commendation and was called righteous. It isn't enough to offer God partial obedience or to learn what to do but then fail to do it. This word "righteous" carries the connotation of justice (in the principle, a decision, or its execution), and a righteous person is one who makes decisions by principle and then follows it up with execution—doing it.

Cain wanted to do it his way. Look back to the end of verse five, where it says it made Cain infuriated that God accepted Abel's sacrifice and that he looked dejected. His face revealed what was in his heart: disgust, disappointment, and anger that making the offering his way was rejected or wasn't enough. Think on this for a moment—what could we call the way Cain responded to God?

Pride.

Cain wanted to be blessed for doing his own thing. God even told Cain how to make it right. God said that if he did right (literally to retrace his steps, consider his ways, and find where he'd gone wrong so he could amend his offering), he would be accepted. If not, he was letting sin into his heart. From the very beginning, God has been showing us mercy.

God warned him!

But I believe that his pride prevented Cain from changing his actions to match God's principles. Cain determined to do it his way, and perhaps he thought that if Abel weren't there, as the only one left standing he'd be the best by elimination. His feelings of anger probably only intensified in the days, weeks, and possibly even months to come as he began to observe the blessings of God manifesting in his brother's life. Cain watched as he worked just as hard as Abel, but everything Abel touched seemed to work, while everything Cain did seemed not to be enough.

Cain's rebellion cost him.

After he had killed his brother, he was expelled from the presence of God (a reflection of how sin separates us from God). He lost his connections, as he had to leave his family and those he knew. He lost his security, and he had no home or covering or safety. But he also lost his harvest—all the hard work he'd done on his fields to make them yield good crops was lost to him because now he wouldn't be there to harvest what he'd worked so hard to plant.

Have you ever felt like this?

If you feel cut off from God and your connections with others, insecure, or that all your hard work yields you nothing, it is time to ask God to examine your heart to see if you are opening yourself to this by not following His ways.

To a significant degree, your decisions determine your future outcomes—your destiny. By aligning your life with the Word of God, you will reap His magnificent and divine rewards. And the best part is that it's never too late to retrace your steps, consider your ways, and find where you've gone wrong.

You can make God's presence and principles your priority—today! You can practice His principles now, even if you have not done so before. The best part about this is that it is never too late to repent and turn around.

I used the word "practice" above very intentionally. It means to carry out or apply a customary way of operation or to learn by repetition. You are always presented with opportunities to practice God's presence, and it is His hope that you will learn, through repetition, to do it right.

Covenant

Abel did not yet have the covenant God later made with His people, but he understood how God operated. And Abel still understood bekhor—that firstfruits offer a promise to come. Abel knew the ways and principles of God and that God made a promise that if he gave God the first, He would bless the rest.

And God counted it as righteousness.

One of the most interesting connections of firstfruits is the link with the covenant God established with His people. In

Exodus 22, God tells the Children of Israel not to delay bringing offerings from their granaries, wine vats, cattle, sheep—and even their sons. With their children, they sacrificed a redeeming animal or paid a price to redeem their first-born son. And they dedicated all their sons to God through circumcision.

Though we use this word, "circumcision," to the Hebrews, it's briyth, which means "covenant." This is the Hebrew way of demonstrating that their sons, the best their society had to offer, are dedicated to God and set apart for Him, just as they are as a people.

Circumcision was more than just a sign of being a Hebrew, for there were Hebrews before God instituted circumcision with Abraham. It's a sign of the covenant.

God is a covenant-making and covenant-keeping God, and the Bible is a book full of agreements. The Old Testament covenants described the transactions between God and men in great detail and were binding legal agreements. It was God's law, His order, and His ways laid out so He could bless His people.

But God used this to show us that we could not keep all the details of the law and needed a Savior, and so He sent Jesus to create an unconditional covenant where God obligates Himself, in grace, to bless His people. Not because of our deeds—because we could never fulfill all the law—but because of Jesus' willing sacrifice. He kept the law for us because we are unable to do so.

Our covenant was legally and permanently secured in Jesus, and God cannot and will not deny Himself. He remains faithful to His covenantal Word.

But receiving this covenant requires that we receive Christ, and I don't believe that we can fully claim our promised inheritance until we know who we are in Christ. Knowing "who" we are in Christ is knowing what we have in Christ.

We All Need Help

We want to choose what is right, but on our own seem unable to honor God's ways and principles. We need help. Paul wrote of this problem. Take a moment, pick your own Bible, and look up Romans 7:14-20 to get the whole context of what he had to say. We resume in verse 21:

I have discovered this principle of life—that when I want to do what is right, I inevitably do what is wrong. I love God's law with all my heart. But there is another power within me that is at war with my mind. This power makes me a slave to the sin that is still within me. Oh, what a miserable person I am! Who will free me from this life that is dominated by sin and death? Thank God! The answer is in Jesus Christ our Lord.

(Romans 7:21-25a NLT)

Without help, we cannot live by God's principles. I want you to understand the importance of obedience, but I also want you to know that without Christ's power working within you, enabling you, you cannot keep the law, or even observe just the principle of firstfruits, and earn God's blessing.

We all need Jesus, for with Him all things are possible.

The Ultimate Firstfruit

The principle of firstfruits is so powerful that Adam's sin dictated the pattern for all humanity since the fall. Paul writes, "When Adam sinned, sin entered the world. Adam's sin brought death, so death spread to everyone, for everyone sinned" (Romans 5:12 NLT).

Paul contrasts Adam and Jesus in Romans 5, and I strongly suggest you pick up your Bible and read from verse 12 to the end. For our purposes, I want to focus on a particular part—that

Jesus is the last Adam. Paul continues: "Now Adam is a symbol, a representation of Christ, who was yet to come. But there is a great difference between Adam's sin and God's gracious gift. For the sin of this one man, Adam, brought death to many. But even greater is God's wonderful grace and his gift of forgiveness to many through this other man, Jesus Christ" (Romans 5:14b-15 NLT).

God knew that we could not counteract the weight of Adam's fall on our own through obedience to the law. And so God brought fulfillment to the Old Covenant and offered a new firstfruits offering, for us, so that we could be right with Him. In 1 Corinthians, Paul writes,

> *But now Christ is risen from the dead, and has become the firstfruits of those who have fallen asleep. For since by man came death, by Man also came the resurrection of the dead. For as in Adam all die, even so in Christ all shall be made alive. But each one in his own order: Christ the firstfruits, afterward those who are Christ's at His coming.*
> *(1 Corinthians 15:20-23 NKJV)*

God loved us too much to leave us dead in our sins under Adam's curse, so Jesus established a new order or a new pattern. Because He was the Firstborn of God, a Firstfruit, He could form a new pattern for humankind that revoked the curse Adam's sin had brought.

James writes, "Of His own will He brought us forth by the word of truth, that we might be a kind of firstfruits of His creatures" (James 1:18 NKJV). Sin entered through one man eating the firstfruits and setting the destiny for the whole human race, but thanks to Jesus, that future has been changed.

We are now partakers of the divine nature of God. In Christ, we are shareholders in His authority! And because we are being transformed into His image instead of conformed to the world, we can reproduce after our kind. Jesus is the firstborn, but we are joint-heirs with Christ, and He is the firstborn among many brothers and sisters in Christ.

Jesus set a new pattern for all humanity, and the law of the seed that God started in the Garden of Eden still proves true today: every seed produces after its kind. Jesus, the ultimate firstfruits offering, died, was buried, and rose again as the first part of a harvest of life that goes on through us.

God doesn't see Adam's sin and the consequences of that ruined firstfruit offering anymore. When He looks at you, He sees the image of His Son because of the blood He shed and the New Covenant we're under.

We who abide in Him are His disciples, and the truth we know has set us free from the law of sin and death! God's covenant is His law. With that covenant we have everything we need, every promise of God is ours when we apply and stand on His Word.

As Peter wrote to those in exile after the resurrection of Jesus:

> *Grace and peace be multiplied to you in the knowledge of God and of Jesus our Lord; seeing that His divine power has granted to us everything pertaining to life and godliness, through the true knowledge of Him who called us by His own glory and excellence. For by these He has granted to us His precious and magnificent promises, so that by them you may become partakers of the divine nature, having escaped the corruption that is in the world by lust.*
> *(2 Peter 1:2-4, NASB)*

Simply, we have the right to be the recipient of these through our obedience, thanks to Jesus, the ultimate Firstfruit.

Be a "Doer"

You may have heard the old preacher joke that there were five frogs on a log. One decides to jump off. So how many frogs are left? The answer, of course, is five—because deciding something is not the same as doing.

A few pages ago, I used the word "abide." I was referring to John 15, where Jesus explains how we must be connected to Him. He said,

> *I am the vine, you are the branches. He who abides in Me, and I in him, bears much fruit; for without Me you can do nothing. If anyone does not abide in Me, he is cast out as a branch and is withered; and they gather them and throw them into the fire, and they are burned. If you abide in Me, and My words abide in you, you will ask what you desire, and it shall be done for you. By this My Father is glorified, that you bear much fruit; so you will be My disciples.*
> *(John 15:5-8 NKJV)*

When He says, "Abide," Jesus isn't referring to hearing Him preached about in church. He doesn't mean, "Learn a lot about me." He wants us to be transformed by Him and to be acting on what is happening in our hearts so that others will see the fruit we bear as His disciples. God wants us to be fruitful so that He may be glorified on the earth.

The hard reality is that you can intellectually understand what I'm telling you about firstfruits and the principles God has established. You can know that you are a living, breathing seed that can reproduce just like the firstborn from the dead, Jesus.

But it will not change your life until, empowered by the Holy Spirit, you honor God with your obedience and do what He says.

God desires our obedience, not our sacrifices. He wants to bless you, to remake your life to resemble Christ's, and to reproduce this new life through you in the lives of others.

But none of this will happen without your obedience—without you doing.

I could list dozens upon dozens of blessings promised in the Word that God sincerely desires to get to you. The abundant life that God has for you is just waiting for you to take a step, to make a transition, and to walk by faith in the truth of His Word.

James writes these words—the last Scripture I will give you in this section and possibly the one, above all others, I want you to grasp:

> *But be doers of the word, and not hearers only, deceiving yourselves. For if anyone is a hearer of the word and not a doer, he is like a man observing his natural face in a mirror; for he observes himself, goes away, and immediately forgets what kind of man he was. But he who looks into the perfect law of liberty and continues in it, and is not a forgetful hearer but a doer of the work, this one will be blessed in what he does. (James 1:22-25 NKJV).*

You must become a "doer" of the Word and not just a "hearer" only. When you do, the principles of God are just waiting to bless you, and firstfruits is just the first of many.

Chapter 5

Why We Have Feasts

God created divine appointments with His people throughout the Old Testament. It's important to understand that the Israel did not have the constant indwelling presence of the Holy Spirit like New Testament Christians do. Instead, they had to meet with God at specific times, in specific places, in specific ways. These ways were the biblical feasts.

God gave specific instructions regarding these holy days and how to observe them and honor Him. These biblical feasts were opportunities for deeper communion and blessings where God could interact with His children more intimately. They were special occasions or God's own "holy days"—His holidays built around the cycles of worshiping Him.

Opportunities to draw near to God, even today, are holy days. Though we are not under the law, the principles behind God's feasts continue through today and provide us with a choice. We can seek to observe these principles out of a legalistic attitude—because we "have to"—or out of obedience and a heart attitude that says we "get to." Reminding ourselves of God's ways is for our benefit, not His. He seeks to bless us as we honor Him.

I think of it as being a little bit like Valentine's Day or an anniversary. I have noticed that some people treat "holidays" like Valentine's Day or anniversaries as a chore—something they have to do. We've all seen the humorous examples of men who feel coerced into spending money on their dates or who are fearful of forgetting an anniversary, but this is just an illustration of how easy it is for something that should be a celebration to become an obligation.

We take opportunities such as Valentine's Day or an anniversary to celebrate love, commitment, relationship, and being with the one we love. When we embrace these chances to come together, we have opportunities to build intimacy in a relationship and to express our love and commitment for one another.

I love getting together with my husband to celebrate special events together. Sometimes we go to a restaurant that is nicer than we would usually visit, consciously don't talk about the ordinary things of everyday life, and often exchange well-thought-out gifts. We take special occasions as opportunities to express our love.

I hope you've had the chance to experience a beautiful evening with your special someone. But now, instead of your spouse, imagine that this amazing date is with your Lord and Savior. Think of all the feelings of a special dinner date and understand that this is how God wants you to feel about appointments with Him.

This intimacy is why He instituted feasts, and it's why we should observe the principles even today—because they're opportunities to express love.

Three Elements of Biblical Feasts

God designated seven feasts for the His people (see Leviticus 23), and these feasts were opportunities for greater intimacy with God. They were a chance to express their love for God and God to show His people reminders of His faithfulness and love.

I want us to look at three Hebrew words used for these special days that each convey an idea we need to grasp. The first is mo'ed, which means a season or an appointed time. Just as the Creator made the sun, moon, and stars for time and seasons in Genesis 1, He also selected dates on the calendar when His people got to set time apart with Him away from the ordinary business of life. Feasts are appointments set ahead of time to meet with God, which is a principle we can and should keep embracing today.

The second concept I want us to understand is mikrah, which is a convocation, a sacred assembly, or rehearsal of God's past, present, and future acts. Each Old Testament feast is designed to remember something the Lord did or to foreshadow an aspect of the ministry of Jesus. Remember, the entire Old Testament was just setting the stage for the Savior, and Jesus fulfilled all of the prophecies while He was on earth, many of which tie into the feast calendar.

Third is the word chag, which is a festive celebration. Chag sets the tone for how we think about meeting with God; these appointments with God are to be festive, happy occasions. They were full of eating and drinking and dancing and singing—they were parties! God had His people meet with Him to celebrate what He had or was going to do with parties full of celebrating and remembering. I believe this tells us something important about the attitude God has about these meetings and reinforces what I said earlier: we don't observe these principles because we have to but because we get to. Not only did God design His celebrations to be happy occasions, but He also built in principles of great rewards for those who celebrated joyfully and voluntarily.

What does this tell us about our God? And what does it imply about how we should continue to observe the principles He founded these feasts on? I believe that it tells us that we are completely wrong if our perception of God is that He is a cosmic killjoy, sitting up in heaven and just itching to catch us messing up. These feasts seasons weren't opportunities for His people to act more self-righteous and stiff; they were chances to celebrate and enjoy God's blessings and honor Him for His goodness in their lives.

The Seven Feasts

God masterfully orchestrated the sequence and timing of His appointments with His people by designating seven feasts during three feast seasons: Passover, Pentecost, and Atonement (Tabernacles). They represented three major links between God and His covenant children.

1. *The first was the Feast of Passover, which not only commemorated how the angel of death passed over the Hebrew homes in Egypt but also points to Christ as our Passover Lamb (see Exodus 11 and 12).*
2. *The second was the Feast of Unleavened Bread, which points to Jesus as the Bread of Life (see John 6:35).*
3. *Next was the Feast of Firstfruits, which guides us directly to the Savior (see 1 Corinthians 15:2-23).*
4. *The fourth was the Feast of Pentecost. Jesus sent the Holy Spirit to bear witness of the Savior during Pentecost (see Acts 2:1-4).*
5. *Fifth came the Feast of Trumpets, which reveals the soon coming Savior (see 1 Thessalonians 4:16).*
6. *Sixth was the Feast of Atonement, a guided understanding of how the Word became flesh (see Romans 5:8-15).*
7. *Seventh and last was the Feast of Tabernacles. This showed us the Creator's plan to send His Son to*

renew fellowship with us and establish His authority, ownership, and rein (see John 1:14).

Each feast or divine appointment, especially Passover, demonstrates how everything in the Old Testament pointed to the cross and beyond. They illustrated supernatural truths, blessings, and principles for us today as surely as they pointed to the future and commemorated the past for the Israelites. They were all built on the foundation of God's blood covenant with humanity.

The difference between the Hebrew people and Christians is that remission of sins was accomplished by shedding the blood of sacrificial animals during the Old Testament, but we are under a better covenant. Jesus' blood was poured out for us, once and for all time, and because of His blood, there are significant benefits for you!

Let's look at them together.

Chapter 6

The First Feast of the Lord

Passover is the first feast of the Lord. It is the foundational feast or first feast season of the Hebrew calendar. Passover commemorates the Israelites' exodus from hundreds of years of slavery in Egypt and the redemption of a newborn nation, a people belonging to the Lord. Sprinkling the blood of a Passover lamb on the doorposts rescued the Israelites from the destroying angel that struck down the firstborn in Egypt, but what's exciting is how God used this to foreshadow the blood that Jesus would pour out for us on a particular feast hundreds of years later.

Our word "Passover" comes from the Hebrew word paach, which means to extend the arms or wings over one, protecting them. So Passover isn't so much about "passing by" as passing so as to shield over for protection. This is exactly what the blood on the doorposts of the Israelites' homes did—it acted as a shield or protection.

Passover has been celebrated annually since the time of Moses since God established that it was to be kept forever in Exodus 12:14. We will go over the story of Passover from Exodus chapter 12 shortly, but first I would like to give you some of the backgrounds of how the Israelites found themselves enduring four hundred years of slavery in Egypt.

A Brief History of Passover

I would like to frame up this feast by giving you a brief history lesson. At the end of the book of Genesis, Joseph dies. He had the favor of Pharaoh for how his wisdom and insight into Pharaoh's dreams had not only enabled Egypt to survive but to prosper during the seven years of famine.

However, a day came when the pharaohs of Egypt no longer remembered Joseph. Just as Joseph's brothers had sold him into slavery in Egypt, within a few generations their descendants became ruthlessly enslaved by the same nation to which they had sold their brother. The Egyptians were hard and cruel taskmasters over the Israelites, and this abusive slavery shaped the narrative of Passover.

As the Egyptians forced the Israelites to labor for them and build their cities, God's people continued to multiply. In fact, Exodus says, "But the more the Egyptians oppressed them, the more the Israelites multiplied and spread, and the more alarmed the Egyptians became. So the Egyptians worked the people of Israel without mercy" (Exodus 1:12-13 NLT).

The people of Egypt were so afraid of the growing Israelite population that they decided to take extreme measures. Pharaoh decreed that all the baby boys were to be killed, and when the Hebrew midwives would not kill the baby boys, he had his soldiers do it.

Moses was born into this environment of genocide. Against all the odds, God preserved his life because Moses' mother would not simply let the Egyptians kill her son. Ironically, Moses is raised by Pharaoh's daughter in the household of his people's worst enemy. Moses' name means "drawing out." God brought him out of death, and later He would bring Moses out of a life of ease in Pharaoh's court to prepare him to be God's instrument to deliver His people.

The call on Moses' life was to free God's people, and his first instinct was to do this on his own. When he saw a Hebrew being beaten by an Egyptian slave master, he took matters into his hands and murdered the Egyptian.

The Word tells us that vengeance is the Lord's, and it was not God's plan to free His people by having Moses murder an Egyptian. God had a plan that would bring Him glory. Moses fled Egypt, running into the desert, where he lived for decades as a shepherd until he received God's call to return to Egypt from a burning bush. God had decided it was time for Him to execute judgment on the Egyptians, and He chose Moses to speak for Him.

Moses had changed during his time in the desert, the blowing sands removing his pride and arrogance until God was able to work through his weaknesses. Without so much "Moses" in the way, God delivered ten plagues upon the Egyptians—each representing the ten "gods" that the Egyptians served—each seemingly worse than the last. And we get the story of Passover from that tenth, and worst, plague.

A Fresh Start

God revealed to Moses and Aaron that He had more in mind for this tenth plague than the others. He told them how He would deliver the Israelites from it, and He gave them so much more setup than with the other plagues. This wasn't merely delivering the final blow to Pharaoh. The tenth plague, the context in which Passover occurred, was to be a fresh start—a reboot—for His people. In Exodus 12, we read,

While the Israelites were still in the land of Egypt, the Lord gave the following instructions to Moses and Aaron:

"From now on, this month will be the first month of the year for you. Announce to the whole community of Israel that on the tenth day of this month each family must choose a lamb or a young goat for a sacrifice, one animal for each household. If a family is too small to eat a whole animal, let them share with another family in the neighborhood. Divide the animal according to the size of each family and how much they can eat. The animal you select must be a one-year-old male, either a sheep or a goat, with no defects.
(Exodus 12: 1-5 NLT)

God changed the Hebrew calendar to make this the first day of their new year. Just stop and consider that for a moment: Passover is so significant that God restarted their entire calendar system based on it. That is how important His redemption and deliverance is!

God gave specific instructions about how Hebrews were to take care of the sacrifice until the appointed time. He even told them how they were to cook it and eat it. But there was another aspect that was even more significant and deeply symbolic. God told them, "And they shall take of the blood, and strike it on the two side posts and on the upper door post of the houses" (Exodus 12:7 KJV).

The shedding of blood is incredibly significant throughout the Bible, and the fantastic symbolic gesture that God had them do by spreading the blood on the doorposts of their houses paints us a picture of how Jesus' blood would be shed for us. This Passover, the first one, just set the template. God had an even grander plan for this feast that He would not reveal for hundreds of years.

Having told them how to prepare and handle, cook, and eat the sacrifice, and that they were to spread the blood liberally in a very obvious way, God goes on to set the stage for what He's about to do in Egypt. He has Moses prepare the people for their deliverance—He wanted them ready to move when He moved. God tells them to eat their meal fully dressed, with their sandals on their feet and their walking sticks in their hands. He wanted His people ready.

God explains that He will pass through the land of Egypt and strike down every firstborn son and firstborn male animal in the entire area as a judgment against all the gods of Egypt. Remember, Pharaoh had killed all the firstborn sons of Israel, trying to contain God's people through an act of genocide. Pharaoh had sowed blood, and he would now reap a terrible harvest.

The blood on the doors of God's people would be a sign marking clearly who is His, and when God saw that blood covering over them, He would pass by, and the plague of death would not touch them. All of Israel had wept when their sons were killed; but now, if Pharaoh didn't relent, all of Egypt would cry for the loss of not only the firstborn boys but even the firstborn animals.

I love something about God: even before He had even done a thing, He gave instructions that they were to remember this day each year, from generation to generation, as a special celebration and festival to the Lord—an "everlasting ordinance" (Exodus 12:14). In fact, God spends more time telling Moses and Aaron about how to commemorate the event than He does explaining what's going to happen on that momentous night! He hasn't even done it yet, and He's already telling them how to remember it forever after!

Freeing His people in a dramatic, earth-shaking fashion was important to God. He was doing a great work for His people, and before He even did a thing, He instructed that they would commemorate what He was about to do forever afterward. (Don't you love God's confidence! What would happen if you could capture this sense of certainty from your God and used it to boost your faith?)

God does not just redeem His people and free them from slavery; He does it in such a way that Passover changes all of history.

Passover showed that the Lord makes a distinction between His people and those who are not His. But there can be no saving or redemption without the shedding of blood. So at Passover, the blood of the sacrificial lamb marked who His was. And whoever was marked as His by blood was saved; the others experienced the tenth plague, and all of Egypt cried out in mourning.

A Better Sacrifice

Okay, now I want to prepare you for a growing understanding of the principle that God was instituting at Passover because it is so amazing.

As good as the sacrifice was that God used to redeem and free His people—so good that it demanded they change their very calendar system to commemorate it—we have a better sacrifice.

Think on this: the blood of a lamb marked the doors of the Israelite homes, and it told an avenging angel not to touch them. The blood of Christ marks our hearts, and it tells the enemy and accuser of the brethren "hands off." Passover commemorated the Israelites being freed from four hundred years of slavery; Jesus' death and resurrection signified the end of humanity's slavery to sin. Christ's redeeming, purchasing blood delivered us not from Egyptians but the power of the prince of this world!

We will shortly look at the blood of Christ in more detail, but for now, I want you to begin simply to soak in the significance, and the parallels, of Passover. Because if you think what I just told you is good, just wait!

Chapter 7

God of Covenant

God set up what He was about to do at Passover with instructions about how His people were to prepare for it, but He told them in advance that what He was doing would change everything for them. It would be so significant, in fact, that it literally would change their entire calendar—Passover would now mark the first month of their year.

The first Passover changed everything that came after.

But God was just warming up.

God responded to the cry of His people and remembered His covenant with Abraham, Isaac, and Jacob because He is a covenant-keeping God. He raised up Moses out of the midst of genocide, where Pharaoh was killing the Hebrew baby boys, and turned him into the leader His people needed before He sent Moses back to Egypt to demand their freedom.

The tenth plague changed everything—so much so that God restarted the Hebrew calendar to commemorate how He delivered His people to freedom. God was giving His people a new beginning.

It was their "moment."

The tenth plague marked the end of their slavery, but it also denoted a new beginning. It may seem obvious, but consider that one thing must always come to an end for another to begin.

Our crisis moments are often turning point opportunities to create decisive moments, which is why it's so important not to miss a moment God has appointed for you. You can let your circumstances rule you, or you can choose to be forever changed by your moment.

Passover was Israel's moment.

Show Up for Your Moment

When we had just started the church in Tampa, we took our small staff on a "retreat" to a dude ranch to reward them for all their hard work and to bond together as a team. We were to be there three days, but on the first day I received a phone call and invitation to go to Louisville, Kentucky, where an international evangelist was hosting a revival meeting. He felt it was urgent and necessary for me to be there. I prayed and decided to leave my staff retreat on the last day and go to this meeting in Kentucky.

When I arrived, they sat me next to a woman in the ministry whom I'd admired and respected for years. She asked how things were going in Tampa with our newly-formed church. I couldn't stop talking, telling her about the goodness of God and how we had started in the inner city, reaching those in great need with the Gospel and very practically meeting their needs with food, clothing, and medical care. I was sharing story after story of those who received salvation.

She began to tear up and asked if I thought we could do that in Los Angeles, her hometown. She told me how she'd taken Bibles to China and fed the poor in India but never in her back yard.

This was right after the riots that had stricken LA in 1992. I immediately said, "Yes!" and the next thing I knew, I was on a plane the following Monday morning! When I got there, I helped start an outreach program by the name of Operation Stitches that won over fifty thousand souls to the Lord in just six weeks in the Waverly Gardens/Watts area—the very heart of the gang-ridden inner city of Los Angeles!

Operation Stitches became a massive movement that would eventually train thousands of churches and organizations in how to reach souls and transform the inner cities of America.

Had I not listened to the inner voice of the Holy Spirit at that moment at the dude ranch to go to Kentucky, I don't know if Paula White Ministries would even exist. It was the launching pad for the greater things God had in store! When God has a moment for you, you have to show up.

Details Matter in the Moment

Moments and little details matter to God. We can see it in creation. Moving the Earth just a relatively small average distance closer to the sun would cause a series of events that would dramatically warm our world; the same with moving it a relatively small distance further away from the sun, cooling the planet. We are a perfect distance from our sun because God does details.

The Earth is not just the right distance, the orbit—which changes in distance from the sun over the course of a year— combines with the way the Earth is tilted on its axis at 23.5 degrees to create our seasons. If we orbited the sun in a perfect circle, or if the Earth was not tilted so correctly on its axis, it would rob us of seasons, air movement in the atmosphere, and ocean currents. I have no idea what would happen if air and water didn't circulate the earth, but I guarantee it would be bad! God knew what our world needed.

Even the ingredients in our atmosphere and oceans are just right—every little detail is perfect—because God loves details, and His details are perfect. Everything He does is according to design; there are no coincidences in His world.

But this is particularly the case when it comes to God's plans for His people. In Revelation 13:8, we read that the Book of Life belongs to the Lamb "slain from the foundation of the world." Before the world was even made, God had planned that His Son, Jesus, called the Lamb of God, would be slaughtered for our sins.

Did you catch that? Go back and read it again if your jaw didn't drop, because it's that good.

Jesus wasn't God's backup plan. Adam's sin didn't catch God by surprise, unprepared, forcing Him to send Jesus to try to clean up the mess. God knew what it would take to make us the Bride of Christ. The Lamb was slain from the foundation of the world—for you and me. God had a plan all along.

God's Plans Are Perfect

God told Moses and Aaron a little in advance that He was going to visit a tenth plague on the Egyptians. He told them weeks ahead that they were to sacrifice a lamb and put its blood on their doors. He told them in advance before He'd done a thing, which they were to commemorate how He passed over them forever and changed their calendar. God foreshadowed what Jesus would do for the world by how He handled Passover. But He knew from the foundations of the world that this was what He was going to do!

God loves details that coincide. It took nine months for Moses to complete the Tabernacle in the wilderness (see Exodus 19:1 and Numbers 19:1-2), and it took nine months to "form" a body for Jesus (who was the true Tabernacle that brought God and man together) in Mary's womb (see Luke 1:26-38). I could go on and on with dates and periods that coincide, but for now, just consider that it was absolutely no accident that Jesus was hung on the cross at Passover, which we're going to talk about in more detail later.

God was working out His eternal—yes eternal (see Ephesians 3:11)—purpose hundreds of years in advance. And what was that plan? "God chose to save us through our Lord Jesus Christ, not to pour out his anger on us" (1 Thessalonians 5:9 NLT).

I love how the Message paraphrase describes God's secret plan of redemption He previewed at the first Passover:

> *Long before he laid down earth's foundations, he had us in mind, had settled on us as the focus of his love, to be made whole and holy by his love. Long, long ago he decided to adopt us into his family through Jesus Christ. (What pleasure he took in planning this!) He wanted us to enter into the celebration of his lavish gift-giving by the hand of his beloved Son.*
> *Because of the sacrifice of the Messiah, his blood poured out on the altar of the Cross; we're a free people—free of penalties and punishments chalked up by all our misdeeds. And not just barely free, either. Abundantly free! He thought of everything, provided for everything we could need, letting us in on the plans he took such delight in making. He set it all out before us in Christ, a long-range plan in which everything would be brought together and summed up in him, everything in deepest heaven, everything on planet earth.*
> *(Ephesians 1:4-10 MSG)*

God's eternal plan was to pour out His Son's blood to free us. Nothing has taken Him by surprise—not Adam's sin, and certainly not any of yours.

Some people have this idea of God as an authoritarian dictator who is out to get us like a kid who loves to step on ants. They feel He's so high-and-mighty and pious and intolerant that His only joy is smashing us whenever we mess up.

But nothing could be further from the truth.

How could it impact how you see yourself, and how you think of God if you let this idea capture your thinking: God planned, from the foundation of the world, to send Jesus to buy your freedom and redeem you from your sins.

He has been orchestrating the details for all eternity to lead up to the moment Jesus died on the cross to pay the price in blood for our sins. Every small event, every feast, every prophecy—they all worked together, in perfect synchronicity and in total harmony, to set the stage for Jesus to be the Lamb of God, sacrificed for the sins of the world.

He did it for you. He did it to turn your captivity around so that you would no longer have to be a slave to sin but could be alive again through Jesus Christ. He did it to give you an abundant life (one that is superior in quality) through Jesus Christ!

Now that is something to celebrate!

God Will Turn Your Captivity Around

Exodus chapter 23 is a revealing passage of Scripture that many Christians have ignored. It focuses on the feasts of the Passover season, and in this text are seven specific blessings of the Passover. Remember, these are principles God established for His people, and before we go on to examine how Jesus is the ultimate Passover blessing for us, I want you to catch these others.

The first Passover blessing for God's people is in Exodus 23:20-21 and 23, where God promises to send an angel before us to protect us and lead us to the destination He has prepared for us. "Behold, I send an Angel before you to keep you in the way and to bring you into the place which I have prepared. Beware of Him and obey His voice; do not provoke Him, for He will not pardon your transgressions; for My name is in Him" (Exodus 23:20-21).

Notice in the new King James Translation that "Angel" and the pronouns "He" and "His" are capitalized. When you see this in the Old Testament, generally it is because Bible scholars feel this refers to a representation of the Son before the Word became flesh and dwelt among us.

God cautions the Israelites to obey His instructions, so again we see the importance of obedience. Many of us grew up with the concept of guardian angels, and I believe it is part of God's character to use His holy messengers to protect His people. However, how much better is it that our Advocate before the Father, Jesus Himself, is the one guarding and protecting His people? I'll take that any day, knowing that Jesus is watching over and taking care of me.

The next promise is that God will contend that those who fight against us. God promises, "If you indeed obey His voice and do all that I speak, then I will be an enemy to your enemies and an adversary to your adversaries" (Exodus 23:22 NKJV). Many Scriptures promise God will oppose those who oppose us. In Old Testament times, this meant natural enemies that would fight and kill His people, but we just as surely have an enemy. The devil is called the enemy of the beloved, the accuser, and many other titles. He has an army of demonic spirits that oppose us. But no matter how he fights us, we have a principle to stand on—if God is for us, who can be against us?

Third, God promises to prosper His people: "So you shall serve the Lord your God, and He will bless your bread and your water" (Exodus 23:25a NKJV). The Word is full of promises about God blessing His people, causing us to prosper as our soul prospers. This Scripture is God promising to bless their most basic needs, but I believe the principle applies to our finances, our possessions, our essential provision, and our spiritual growth. Again, this is a principle—it tells us about the character of our Creator, and here we see that His character is to bless His people. Don't ever doubt that He is a God who delights in blessing His people!

Fourth, God promises to protect them from illness. "I will take sickness away from the midst of you," God tells them in Exodus 23:25b (NKJV). Jesus bore stripes on His back for our healing, accomplishing the redemption for our sins and paying the price for our healing simultaneously on the cross. If you have faith to believe God for salvation, have faith to believe Him for healing, for the same sacrificial act of Christ paid for both. And don't let anyone try to convince you that healing was for another time because it did not end in Jesus' day. The apostles, and then their disciples, frequently saw people healed as part of their ministry. God's healing power is alive and well, and His character tells us He likes to heal us and protect us from disease.

Fifth, God wants us to be fruitful and to live and not die—He wants us to have long lives. In Exodus 23:26, we read, "No one shall suffer miscarriage or be barren in your land; I will fulfill the number of your days" (NKJV). One translation reads, "I will give you long, full lives" (NLT). Again, we judge these promises against the whole Word, and we find many other Scriptures with like promises. Paul quotes Deuteronomy in Ephesians when he writes, "'Honor your father and mother,' which is the first commandment with promise: 'that it may be well with you and you may live long on the earth'" (Ephesians 6:2-3 NKJV). He desires us to enjoy long, fruitful lives on the earth.

The sixth Passover promise is that He desires to bring success to His people. God promised them the land, but we read, "I will not drive them out from before you in one year, lest the land become desolate and the beasts of the field become too numerous for you. Little by little I will drive them out from before you, until you have increased, and you inherit the land" (Exodus 23:29-30 NKJV). God could've done it instantly (like we often want Him to) or even in a single year, but instead, He gave them the victory progressively. They had to do the work and obey Him, walking in His ways, and as they did so, they increased and inherited the land.

However, it should be noted that when they did not do it His way and obey Him; they left Canaanite tribes in place that should never have given them problems again but did. Again, we see the importance of obedience.

Finally, the seventh promise of Passover God gave to His people was that they would receive His inheritance. God tells them, "And I will set your bounds from the Red Sea to the sea, Philistia, and from the desert to the River. For I will deliver the inhabitants of the land into your hand, and you shall drive them out before you" (Exodus 23:31 NKJV). God had promised them the whole Promised Land, and He would see that they got it! As we read above, God knew what they could handle, and He gave them the inheritance as they had the maturity to possess it.

Let's not ignore the final verses of this chapter, however. These promises come with a cautionary statement: "You shall make no covenant with them, nor with their gods. They shall not dwell in your land, lest they make you sin against Me. For if you serve their gods, it will surely be a snare to you" (Exodus 23:32-33 NKJV). These final instructions were nothing new; they were the same commands God gave them on Mount Sinai. They were to have no other gods before Him, and right here God explains what will happen if they did not obey. He told them how to bask in His blessings and what would happen if they didn't do it His way.

A Covenant-Keeping God

God is a covenant-keeping God, and He desires to set each one of us free from our captivity to sin. He has promised us a great inheritance—every spiritual blessing through His Holy Spirit. We have the principle behind each of these Passover blessings operating for us as the spiritual children of Abraham, but we do not acquire them on our merit.

Jesus bought and paid for the new covenant by which we received all of God's promises with His blood. In the next chapter, I want to walk you through how He was the ultimate Passover Sacrifice for us because God did not limit His promised blessings to the physical descendants of Abraham. That was just the start! Everything we have as New Testament Christians is better in every way under the new covenant, so any blessing that God promised them was only a hint of what we can experience through Christ.

It's time to learn about the ultimate Passover Lamb because He takes the first one, and all those good promises we just read, to a whole new level.

Chapter 8

The Ultimate Passover Lamb

I don't know about you, but way back when I first picked up a Bible, I used to read it as though it were two separate pieces. There were the nice historical bits, some fascinating stories, and a lot of things I didn't understand in the front; and there were the most vivid events of the New Testament in the back. We often tell new believers to stick to the New Testament, setting them up to treat the Bible as two separate pieces instead of parts of the same whole.

For a short time, I failed to connect the two, which is a big mistake.

The way I would like to help you bring the two together is by asking a simple question: what feast did Jesus come to Jerusalem to celebrate even though the Pharisees were plotting to kill Him?

The answer, of course, is Passover.

We can easily "Christianize" the setting of the Gospels, thinking of Palm Sunday and Easter as the events surrounding Jesus' crucifixion and resurrection, but that's only partially correct, and it doesn't take Hebrew prophetic history into account. It's important to understand history and when the Church started celebrating Easter, Palm Sunday, Christmas, and all our other "Christian holidays." It probably will be quite eye-opening to you and surprising as you put it all in context. The

Early Church always kept God's feast seasons. These were divine appointments set by God Himself.

The context of Jesus death and resurrection was that of the feast of Passover.

Jesus did not come into a vacuum. He didn't arrive on a blank slate. He was Jewish, having grown up with all the traditions, feasts, and rules. He arrived on the scene with the table set for God to fulfill His Old Testament promises and all the foreshadowing He had been planning for thousands upon thousands of years.

When I used to think of Passover, I would think of matzoh balls I saw in the grocery store. The whole concept that Passover could have significance for me as a Christian was a foreign idea for many years, as it is to many believers.

All the details we have learned about God foreshadowing Jesus' sacrifice on the cross in the last few chapters came together at the end of His ministry. Jesus wasn't in Jerusalem for "Easter." He was there for Passover—to be the ultimate Passover sacrifice at the most significant Passover celebration ever.

We have seen that God designed Passover to foretell the coming of the Messiah in a physical way. Jesus would die as the Passover Lamb for the whole word and fulfill the prophetic mantle as the Lamb of God.

But now let's go a little deeper as we learn about God's nature through how He fulfilled this feast for us.

Palm Sunday

Take a moment to reconsider all you think you know about Palm Sunday with the knowledge that it's leading up to Passover. Try not to think about it as a modern-day Christian; think about it like Jesus would have—as a Jew. He knew what He was about to do, and He understood He was about to become the Lamb for the Passover sacrifice.

What we call "Palm Sunday" began a week of agonies for our Savior. Jews had come to Jerusalem from all over the surrounding countryside for the feast of Passover, which we now know was the beginning of their new year. It marked the end of the old and the beginning of the new—but no one could have foreseen how important this Passover was.

God was about to make everything new. Everything. This particular Passover wasn't about just restarting the Hebrew calendar; God was going to reset the entire world.

Let's set the stage a little by taking a look in the Gospel of John where we can read about the week before Jesus' death. Perhaps you may not have paid attention to the context John gives us in chapter 12, but let's look at it now.

We read, "Six days before the Passover, Jesus came to Bethany, where Lazarus was who had been dead, whom He had raised from the dead" (John 12:1 NKJV). When the people heard He was there, they flocked to see Jesus and Lazarus, whose resurrection was inspiring many people to believe in Jesus.

"The next day a great multitude that had come to the feast, when they heard that Jesus was coming to Jerusalem, took branches of palm trees and went out to meet Him, and cried out: 'Hosanna! "Blessed is He who comes in the name of the Lord!" The King of Israel!'" (John 12:12-13 NKJV). The people are quoting a messianic Psalm here, 118:26, so every indication is that they had high hopes for what Jesus was about to do.

They understood that God was about to move, and understanding produces movement. The people realized something was about to happen, and they went out to meet Him.

In some ways, they understood principles that many Christians do not. The Greek translated into "went out" is "to issue." Think of ancient times when a ruler would issue a decree, as Caesar did, sending Joseph and Mary to Bethlehem.

The people went out to meet with Jesus because they expected something from Him. They were expecting a "God moment," that something amazing was going to happen. They understood that something was going on because those who'd seen Lazarus raised from the dead were talking about it, so they took a step and issued forth an order to encounter God and get a result.

We as modern-day believers need to practice gaining understanding and then issuing forth so we too can experience our God moments and get results. However, the results we experience have already been accomplished through the death, burial, and resurrection of Jesus Christ, which provides everything we need—spiritually and naturally. By faith, we must manifest the victory in our lives, which was secured in Christ. The Jews were waiting for Jesus to do something—for their God moment to result in something miraculous.

But God has already done the miraculous for us. He did it by raising Jesus from the dead! Jesus has already accomplished His greatest work, that of the cross, and now we only must reach up and accept that for which He has already paid! Our salvation, our healing, our joy, our prosperity, our protection, our deliverance, our peace, patience, kindness, longsuffering, and every other spiritual blessing have already been bought and paid for by the blood of Christ!

These people didn't live there yet; Jesus hadn't done it yet. But they had expectation—they knew something was coming. They knew they needed to issue forth out of their homes because they knew He was coming. They knew they were about to enter into a place and time of results.

We read in Matthew 21:10-11, "And when He had come into Jerusalem, all the city was moved, saying, 'Who is this?' So the multitudes said, 'This is Jesus, the prophet from Nazareth of

Galilee'" (NKJV). This word, "moved" means "to rock or vibrate sideways to and fro"—Jesus was shaking the city, because when God shows up, things begin to move! Eternity was invading the earthly, it was shaking all Jerusalem, and the people could feel it.

When God is moving, we need to have the understanding to position ourselves to experience His exceedingly great power toward us who believe so that we can see movement in our lives because of His mighty power. These people didn't have the finished work of Christ; they were just looking forward with expectation because they'd seen Lazarus raised. We have the Scriptures that spell it out for us, so we should believe in faith and obey; when we do, we will see the strongholds in our lives rocked and moved—and broken.

We read, "Many in the crowd had seen Jesus call Lazarus from the tomb, raising him from the dead, and they were telling others about it. That was the reason so many went out to meet him—because they had heard about this miraculous sign" (John 12:17-18 NLT). God was doing something, starting a movement on that Palm Sunday. The whole city could feel it, and they were about to open up their mouths about it and say something profound.

Hosanna—Save Now

The people had gathered to see Jesus because they had heard about Him from those who had seen His miraculous sign of raising Lazarus from the dead. Those who were with Him had spread the word, and their testimony had caused other people to get in position to see God's purpose fulfilled.

I want to go back and focus in on something that the crowd said during Jesus' triumphal entry, which we just read. They shouted, "'Hosanna! "Blessed is He who comes in the name of the Lord!" The King of Israel!'" (John 12:13 NKJV).

Amazingly, this is a word that had never been recorded in Scripture before. But the Pharisees understood what this word meant. They knew that the people were speaking prophetically because of this word. The implications were that He would do that which He said he would do: that if they tore down His Temple, it would be raised up in three days.

What the Pharisees perhaps didn't understand is that the people had to say "Hosanna!" because they were inspired by God, fulfilling His prophecy. The word "Hosanna" means "save now." The people were uttering a prophetic praise that goes beyond "hallelujah" because the word "hallelujah" is the praise for what God has done.

"Hosanna" is a praise to God for what He is about to do! It is a prophetic phrase that brings your future into alignment with the revelation of God.

Do you remember me telling you that the people were shouting a prophetic Psalm? I want you to read it now in the context of the verse that comes before it: "Save now, I pray, O Lord; O Lord, I pray, send now prosperity. Blessed is he who comes in the name of the Lord! We have blessed you from the house of the Lord" (Psalm 118:25-26 NKJV).

Hosanna—save now. They were calling what was not into existence through their words. He hadn't done it yet, but if they did not cry out the stones would (see Luke 19:40)!

This is why we don't just thank God for what He has done. We prophetically praise Him for what He is doing and about to do! If you are only praising God for the things He has brought you through, you are missing so much of the picture. His people, the nation of Israel, were bringing about God's purpose on the earth for His Son, Jesus Christ.

The cross you bear—your trials, your troubles, your pains,

all of it—will endure for only a brief time. It will hurt for a while, but God is doing something in your life! "And we know that all things work together for good to those who love God, to those who are the called according to His purpose" (Romans 8:28 NKJV). You're still alive, and that is a reason to thank Him.

But don't stop there! Speak, "Hosanna! Save now!" to your life. Tell yourself prophetically that God is moving, shaking up your life, and that amazing things are going to happen. Praise Him now for what you do not yet see.

That is what we call faith.

The people gave voice to it during Jesus' triumphal entry, and the results of Him willingly shedding His blood for all of us to continue to reverberate throughout history.

Chapter 9

The Blood of Jesus

In ancient days the people would have welcomed a conquering hero by laying their clothes and palm branches on the road before him. Great generals of Rome or other victorious nations came home to the people waving palm branches in a triumphant procession. People would cheer for the victor, celebrating that their champions had won out over the enemy.

Palm trees had many symbolic meanings, including being a sign of water—which, in the Middle East, means life—and being a symbol of beauty and prosperity. In a way, they represented life, so as people would celebrate by spreading palm branches on the main road it was a statement that success in life was visiting.

When I lived in Tampa, we had a beautiful property with timeworn, historically preserved oak trees. But one year, a hurricane was coming through, and we evacuated ahead of the storm. When we returned, we found that one of our massive, gorgeous, and very old oak trees had split and smashed on the ground. We lost almost every tree in our yard...except for these ugly old palm trees. In the violent wind, they bent and swayed, nearly bending over to touch the earth. I learned they were held in place by an amazingly deep root system so they would bend but not break. The oak trees, while beautiful, did not have a root system that ran as deep or the ability to flex in the storm, and they suffered terribly from the hurricane. God wants us deeply rooted in Him like the palm trees, so when the storms of life hit us, we will still be standing.

The triumphant entry of conquering heroes echoes the way Jesus entered Jerusalem before Passover in the week before His death. The people recognized something was happening, that God was moving. They could feel it in their bones, and they cried out in the welcome—if they hadn't, the very stones would have shouted!

The descendants of Jacob are a prophetic people, and we are the spiritual descendants of the same line, which God founded through Abraham. They felt the movement of God in the very air as Jesus descended from the Mount of Olives on what we call Palm Sunday. They had seen or heard the testimony of how He had raised Lazarus from the dead, and they knew something was about to happen.

They issued forth from their homes and laid branches down along the road, shouting, "Hosanna!" literally, "Save now!" They were speaking a prophetic praise that brings the future into alignment with the revelation of God. God hadn't done it yet— He had not yet restored man into the relationship with Himself through the death of His Son.

But He was about to.

He was about to pay for all of it in blood. He would redeem us by the superior, precious blood of Jesus.

Complete Deliverance

In Revelation 7:9-10, we read,

I looked, and behold, a great multitude which no one could number, of all nations, tribes, peoples, and tongues, standing before the throne and before the Lamb, clothed with white robes, with palm branches in their hands, and crying out with a loud voice, saying, 'Salvation belongs to our God who sits on the throne, and to the Lamb!'

The Lamb this is referring to is Jesus. He is the Lamb of God, sacrificed for the sins of the world. And the scene of His sacrifice was Passover. Jesus is our Passover Lamb.

In the previous chapter, we had been reading in John 12, following Jesus' triumphant arrival into Jerusalem. What we commonly call Palm Sunday was just a precursor to the main event. Following His entrance into Jerusalem, Jesus again faced off with the Pharisees, washed His disciples' feet, was betrayed by Judas, promised the coming of the Holy Spirit, and was taken by a mob on Gethsemane to be crucified. From Palm Sunday till His crucifixion was the final week of Jesus' earthly ministry before His resurrection.

By the end of that week, His blood would be poured out for us, the redemption of mankind—all those who would believe in their hearts that He is the Son of God and confess this with their mouths (see Romans 10:9-10).

Why We Need a Savior

Passover was necessary for the Hebrews because God was about to move and visit one final plague on the Egyptians. Everyone who was not redeemed by blood—the blood of the sacrificial lamb spread on the doorposts of their homes—was visited by the angel of death, and all of the firstborn in Egypt perished. However, because of the blood of an innocent sacrifice, the death angel "passed over" and God protected His people.

Throughout the Old Testament, God's people sacrificed to the Lord during various feasts, but also to cover over or atone for their sins. Once a year, the high priest would offer a blood sacrifice, and an innocent animal would atone for the sins of the people. However, the blood of animals could only cover over the peoples' sin for the year; it couldn't wipe it away.

That took a far greater sacrifice.

When Adam fell, sin entered the world. We have already seen that Jesus was the ultimate Firstfruits sacrifice, but in His death and resurrection on Passover, Jesus became the ultimate Passover sacrifice. But this time, it didn't just reset the Hebrew calendar. We separate our dating system into BC (before Christ) and AD (derived from Latin for "the year of our Lord.")

In other words, Jesus' death reset the entire world!

Under Adam, all people are born into sin and death. We are slaves to sin from the moment of our birth. However, in Jesus Christ, we can all be made alive (see 1 Corinthians 15:22). Those redeemed by Christ are not only recovered from original sin, brought back to life in Christ; we are adopted into God's family through a transfusion of blood—Jesus' blood replacing ours.

That blood was poured out on Calvary by the perfect Lamb of God.

While Israel before the Messiah had to sacrifice again and again each year, Jesus' death on the cross was the one time that paid for all. We read, "For by one offering He has perfected forever those who are being sanctified" (Hebrews 10:14 NKJV). It was a perfect sacrifice that would completely perfect all who put their faith in it. It is complete, lacking nothing.

And it was God's plan all along. Think back: do you remember that Revelation told us the Lamb of God was sacrificed from the foundation of the world? Jesus was not God's Plan B. God is a God of covenants, and God is a God of details. Every detail leading up to Jesus' death as our better Passover sacrifice only pointed to what He would do on the cross.

Hundreds of years before Jesus would be our Passover sacrifice,

Isaiah the prophet wrote, "Surely He has borne our griefs and carried our sorrows; yet we esteemed Him stricken, smitten by God, and afflicted. But He was wounded for our transgressions, He was bruised for our iniquities; the chastisement for our peace was upon Him, and by His stripes we are healed" (Isaiah 53:4-5 NKJV).

Everything you will ever need, both now and in eternity, whether spiritual or physical, financial or physical, emotional or relational, was provided by that one sacrifice. What an awesome God we serve!

The Divine Exchange

Through the sacrifice on the cross, a divine exchange took place that unlocked all of God's provision for us. All of the evil, which justice demanded would cost us eternal death, came upon Jesus. All of the good due to Jesus, earned by His sinless obedience, was made available to us. He, the Passover Lamb, took on Himself the price of our sentence.

Jesus was punished that we might be forgiven.

Jesus was wounded so that we could be healed.

Jesus took on sin, was made into sin so that we could be made righteous because of His righteousness.

Jesus died our death so that we might share His life.

He was made a curse so that we could receive a blessing. He became poor so that we could receive His abundance. He took on our shame so that we could have His glory. He endured our rejection so that we could enjoy His acceptance. Our old man died in Jesus so that a new person could live in us. His blood transfusion changed everything!

But who can receive this amazing gift?

Do you think God only offers this to the perfect people? The poster children for doing kind deeds and keeping their hands clean? Do you think it's just for people who never messed up big time, who avoid hurting others, and who go to church regularly?

No! Here's who can receive this: "And the Spirit and the bride say, 'Come!' And let him who hears say, 'Come!' And let him who thirsts come. Whoever desires, let him take the water of life freely" (Revelation 22:17 NKJV). Every one of us has sinned and fallen short of God's glory, but whoever wants to can come and drink of the Water of Life—Jesus—freely.

You see, all of us have a root problem. "We like sheep have gone astray; We have turned, every one, to his own way; And the Lord has laid on Him the iniquity of us all" (Isaiah 53:6 NKJV). There's a rebel inside each and every one of us.

There's only one remedy for rebels. It's not more Sunday school, it's not learning the golden rule or memorizing Scripture or going to church or trying to be nice.

God's righteousness demands that the solution to rebels is executing them. That's the price of rebellion.

The message of the Gospel, however, is that in His mercy execution took place with Jesus on the cross, and our old man—who we were before Christ—is crucified with Him so that we could be made dead to sin (see Romans 6:6-7).

The One Thing We Must Do

The only thing we have to do to receive this covenant that God designed from the beginning of time, which we can do nothing to deserve, is to accept it and receive it by faith.

Paul writes, "Now if we died with Christ, we believe that we shall also live with Him, knowing that Christ, having been raised from the dead, dies no more. Death no longer has dominion over Him. For the death that He died, He died to sin once for all; but the life that He lives, He lives to God" (Romans 6:8-10 NKJV).

To see your part in all this, look back up at the first line because it shows us the one thing you must do.

You must believe.

We must reckon ourselves dead to sin with Jesus. And when we do, something amazing happens—we are transformed.

Paul writes, "Therefore, if anyone is in Christ, he is a new creation; old things have passed away; behold, all things have become new" (2 Corinthians 5:17 NKJV).

Transformation is what Passover was all about—all things becoming new. It was about your complete deliverance, redemption, and restoration. Although this amazing New Covenant, paid for by Christ's blood, was established before the foundation of the world, it culminated in the climactic moments of the last days of Jesus' life and death, which we usually celebrate from Palm Sunday to Easter. But if we thought a little deeper, I believe that we would celebrate more fully with a feast or divine appointment God instituted and proclaimed should never be forgotten:

Passover.

Chapter 10

The Holiest Day
of the Year

What's the holiest day of the year? For the Children of Israel, there was no question: it was the Day of Atonement. Passover was the day of our personal atonement, the day the Sacrificial Lamb of God died in our place. We have been rescued from death because a perfect substitute sacrifice, Jesus Christ, was found. We are like Isaac, freed from the altar of death. As you applied and received the precious blood of Jesus over the doorpost of your heart, you come to salvation in the New Covenant. Now, let's look at the original purposes of God's most holy day on the Hebrew calendar.

We've been talking about God's appointments with His people and the principles He wanted to share with them through each, and we are entering what's called the Fall Feast Season. Though we have covered some feasts that are truly meaningful, for the Children of Israel no time was holier than the Day of Atonement. But He didn't simply toss His people straight into this holy day; He put it in the midst of a feast season. He set up Atonement with the Feast of Trumpets, a feast designed to help them remember where they'd been and to repent, and then He followed it up with what the Children of Israel just referred to as "the Feast" (or the Feast of Tabernacles).

Atonement, a day of prayer, righteousness, and faith, would

result in the supernatural cleansing of the people. This holiest of days would cleanse or cover the people of their sins. Pretty important, right? Yes—but the promises only started there.

The final feast of the Fall Feast Season was called the Feast Tabernacles, but I like to call it "party time"! It's the season you enter God's unlimited blessing, and I can't wait to share with you what God has shown me about this feast. For the Israelites, it was the time of restoration of all things, and since the same principles—created by the same God—apply to them as to us, when we position ourselves to participate in God's principles, we can experience God's restoration of all things too!

How excited would you be if I told you that now, today, was the season where God wants to restore everything the enemy has taken from your family, your finances, and everything else that the enemy has touched or stolen in your life? That should excite you because all of us have experienced the thief who comes to kill, steal, and destroy. But God wants to give us life, and life abundantly (see John 10:10)!

So if restoration sounds good to you, it's time to learn how to position ourselves and follow God's blueprint so we can get His results. Let's look together at what the Fall Feast Season is all about and how it applies to your life.

The Tabernacles Season

In Deuteronomy chapter 16, the Lord instructs that three times a year the men of Israel were to meet with the Lord at a place He chose. These three meetings were the Feast of Unleavened Bread, the Feast of Weeks, and the Feast of Tabernacles. They were to bring a gift to the Lord, each according to however much God had blessed him.

The Fall Feast Season or Tabernacles Season starts with

the Feast of Trumpets, Rosh Hashanah, which is the call to repentance. God wanted His people to examine their hearts and see the sins and clutter that had accumulated in their lives that were distracting them from Him. It's a time where we examine ourselves to see what is causing us to miss the mark—not just to sin or backslide, but anything that is distracting us from God and to not put Him first in our lives.

Life has a way of burdening us and weighing us down, and fear, stress, worry, and anxiety can creep into our hearts. God knew that His people needed a spiritual tune-up, and they needed to get back on track, so He began the Tabernacles season with a call to repentance. He called us back to Himself, back to basics, back to the core fundamentals of what it means to follow Him as we celebrate the fall feast season. He takes this opportunity to remind us of who we are—blood-bought children of God—and the covenant we have in Him through His Son Jesus Christ!

In the Old Testament, the blowing of the rams horn, the shofar, was the call to repentance. We'll be following along with the prophet Joel as he explains God's principles for His people. We read, "Blow the trumpet in Zion, and sound an alarm in My holy mountain! Let all the inhabitants of the land tremble; for the day of the Lord is coming, for it is at hand" (Joel 2:1 NKJV). The blowing of the horn was a weighty event not to be taken lightly. It was intended to bring trembling and self-reflection, to rid God's people of their complacency and sense of self-contained independence.

But it wasn't all fear and trembling; the same trumpet was a call for Jubilee we read about in Leviticus 25: "And you shall consecrate the fiftieth year, and proclaim liberty throughout all the land to all its inhabitants. It shall be a Jubilee for you; and each of you shall return to his possession, and each of you shall return to his family" (Leviticus 25:10 NKJV).

This word, "return," meant a movement back to the point of departure, to reverse direction, and to go back along a path already traveled. This is the very essence of repentance. Repentance has to do with reconsidering our ways, forsaking them for God's ways. He means to turn around, to think differently afterward, to change one's mind, direction, and purpose.

Repentance was the purpose of the Feast of Trumpets—awe and repentance. God ordered them to take ten days for serious introspection, a period for considering the sins of the previous year and repenting before Yom Kippur, the Day Of Atonement because He was preparing their hearts for what He was going to do.

That has not changed—God still wants to prepare our hearts. The question is, will we obey and be ready for what He wants to do in us?

Repentance

Traditionally, Christians do not have a single day of the year—let alone ten days—where we focus on repentance. I have heard some people say that it's hard to be under the law, but I think that this is an example that our walk under grace calls us to a higher standard than under the law!

Christians do not repent one time a year; we are called to repent daily, regularly. We can repent at any time in prayer because we have a living relationship with God.

With this understanding that God's people had one time a year of corporate repentance, read how Jesus taught His disciples to pray:

> *Our Father in heaven, Hallowed be Your name. Your kingdom come. Your will be done on earth as it is in*

heaven. Give us this day our daily bread. And forgive
us our debts, as we forgive our debtors and do not lead
us into temptation, but deliver us from the evil one.
For Yours is the kingdom and the power and the glory
forever. Amen.
(Matthew 6:9-13 NKJV)

This word, "debts," means our sins. So this is the template that Jesus taught us to use when praying, and it includes repentance in the same breath as asking for provision and protection from the devil. We don't have to wait for a feast season; we can examine our lives on a daily basis, repent, and allow God to correct our course as needed.

The next time you pray—the very next time!—look at your life. How do you treat others? What condition is the condition of your heart? How is your attitude? Is God your priority? Do you have unforgiveness in your heart? If you realize you have something against someone, don't go any further; do what you can to make it right. Forgive and release them. Don't let the enemy get an advantage over you.

Modern Christians lack a proper understanding of what it means to "fear the Lord." The Children of Israel understood. The Feast of Trumpets was designed to set them up for Atonement with awe and reverence, and I strongly encourage you to take some time to study what it means to have the fear of the Lord. Yes, it is the beginning of wisdom, but it is the reverential awe that we as sinners saved by grace should have for a God equally full of righteousness and mercy.

Examine Yourselves

In our freedom, sometimes I think we lose the opportunity to be reminded to clean our spiritual house occasionally. The Feast of Trumpets provided Israel an opportunity to make things right, and their hearts and with one another. It was customary to seek reconciliation with people that you may have wronged during the year, and they had ten days of introspection to help them prepare for the Day of Atonement.

I would like to suggest that we as Christians also have an opportunity for this type of introspection, repentance, and even restitution in relationships: Communion.

Paul tells us we are to examine ourselves before taking communion so that we do not partake of the Lord's Supper unworthily. Paul gives the Corinthian church instructions on how they are to take the Lords Supper. After giving detailed instructions on how to take Communion, he explains how they are to examine themselves.

> *But let a man examine himself, and so let him eat of the bread and drink of the cup. For he who eats and drinks in an unworthy manner eats and drinks judgment to himself, not discerning the Lord's body. For this reason, many are weak and sick among you, and many sleep. For if we would judge ourselves, we would not be judged.*
> *(1 Corinthians 11:28-31 NKJV).*

Remember, the point of learning about these feasts is not so that we hold ourselves responsible for following Hebrew practices exactly. It's to understand the principles behind them and their application to us as New Testament believers. A period of repentance was essential to God for His people then…and it is now.

Every time you pray and every time you take Communion,

be reminded of the Feast of Trumpets and the reverential awe that God's people were to cultivate in their hearts. Take it as an opportunity to examine yourself, as Paul directs, so that instead of eating and drinking judgment or damnation to yourself, you can instead do some spiritual housecleaning and eat and drink blessing.

This sets us up for Atonement, the next step in the process God designed—and trust me, it only gets better from here!

Chapter 11

At One With God

The period of repentance during the Feast of Trumpets was to be ten days of awe that positioned God's people for Yom Kippur, the Day of Atonement. The Day of Atonement is the holiest day in the Hebrew calendar and was to be a day of fasting and honoring God with a sacrificial offering.

I like to think of atonement as meaning simply "at one with God." In Hebrew, it is Yom Kippur, which means covered or redeemed. Its central theme is redemption and repentance because you cannot be one with God without true repentance, which Israel embraced during the Feast of Trumpets we talked about previously.

The Day of Atonement speaks to the act of redemption. It is the holiest day of the feasts, in which the high priest would enter the Holy of Holies, only on this day, to offer blood for the sins of himself and people of Israel. In the book of Hebrews, we see that Jesus Christ was a greater High Priest than those of the Levitical lineage and that He entered Heaven's tabernacle with His blood to make atonement for all the sins ever committed before and after His sacrificial death. He redeemed humanity by His precious blood.

Through redemption, we prepare our hearts for what's to come next. The Day of Atonement speaks of sanctification, a lifestyle in which our flesh enters into alignment with our spirit rather than the other way around. It calls the Church to a life of discipline and purpose in which we understand the seriousness of our sins and what it cost the Lord for the remission of them.

The Sacrifice

The law dictated that there was a blood sacrifice (remember, there can be no remission of sin without the shedding of blood). The high priest would ultimately sprinkle the blood of the sacrifice on a goat that would be put out of the city—the original scapegoat. The blood of this goat would cover over the sins of the people. Leviticus 16 gives us a detailed picture of all that took place on the Day of Atonement.

We know that Jesus Christ became our atonement, and His blood did not cover over our sins—it eradicated them! When a Christian observes the principles behind the Day of Atonement, we are not honoring the blood of a yearly sacrifice; we are honoring Jesus' blood that provides atonement for us.

Jesus' blood redeems us, saves us, covers us, and protects us, which is why no weapon formed against us can prosper. God chooses to see us through lenses tinted by Jesus' blood—He sees us through the blood, seeing His Son's righteousness instead of our filthy rags because the amazing divine exchange that accomplished our atonement.

The Atoning Work of the Cross

As I have mentioned before, we who are in Christ have a better covenant. We know that Jesus Christ made the full and complete atonement for sin for the whole human race by going to the cross. He was the ultimate sin sacrifice!

However, I believe that many Christians have never appropriated the full measure of the atoning work of the cross and the applied blood to the mercy seat of the Ark of the Covenant. That is why divine appointments are so important.

God has set divine appointments with man—His special days when He wants to "meet" with us. They serve as occasions and reminders to honor God and release special blessings assigned to each appointment. It's important to halt in our everyday lives and submit ourselves, dedicating all of our spiritual activities to reviving our relationship with Christ.

The pattern we find in Israel's Day of Atonement is that God has won a real victory over sin and the flesh for His people. We are a royal priesthood, a nation of priests, and we proclaim restoration of the kingdom of God!

All too often, we talk about continuing to wrestle with sin, still dealing with the guilt and condemnation we had experienced before we came to a saving knowledge of Jesus. But while we cannot act perfectly this side of eternity, because of the finished work of Christ, our sins are not just covered over—they are washed away! Jesus' sacrifice did not just deal with our sins for the year, like the blood of a bull or goat. He is the Lamb of God who takes away the sin of the world! The root problem has been dealt with and conquered through Jesus Christ; for all those who put their full trust and dependency in Him, you can find the victory He has for you.

I believe that if we truly understood this, we would walk in freedom instead of feeling guilt. We would know that God sees us through the blood and that we are not working to appease Him but are free to live out an existence where the power of sin has been broken over us through Jesus Christ!

Jesus became our Atonement. God wants to take you to a higher place with Him—seated at the right hand of God in His glory!

The blood of Jesus Christ has redeemed us, and we are not required to follow the formal application of the law or the rabbinic interpretation of Scripture. But we are missing out when we do not create a space in our lives for focusing on Jesus' atoning work and realizing the spiritual opportunities that His blood offers us. The rituals of the Law of Moses helped the Children of Israel understand and align themselves with spiritual truths, and our lives will be blessed and enriched if we allow these principles to impact our faith today.

It's About the Heart

I believe it's vital to honor and obey the principles and patterns that God established in His eternal appointments with His people. We do not make sacrifices—Jesus did that for us— but we can take the time to remember what He did and to let Him position our hearts. Remembering doesn't just have to do with having a memory of or reflecting on something, but its true essence is recognizing what God has done for you.

I love how David puts it in the Psalms, as translated in the Message version: "Going through the motions doesn't please you, a flawless performance is nothing to you. I learned God-worship when my pride was shattered. Heart-shattered lives ready for love don't for a moment escape God's notice" (Psalms 51:16-17 MSG).

It is the attitude of our hearts that makes the critical difference between the Lord accepting our "righteousness" and Him rejecting it. Jesus did the work so that we can be made righteous; we wear it as a robe when we stop and recognize what He did and not take it so much for granted! How often do we fail to think about or appreciate what He has done?

In this ability to quickly forget what God has done for us, we are no different than the Children of Israel. And because God knew our penchant for forgetting even the most miraculous things He has done in our lives, He established the feasts, His divine appointments so that we could remember Him and remember what He has done for us. We could recognize all that He has done and honor Him for it.

Again, I am not trying to call us back to being under the law or back to being under the law or the ritual application of the Old Testament. This isn't about Old Testament rule-keeping; it's about capturing the significance of what Jesus did. He tells us, "Don't misunderstand why I have come. I did not come to abolish the law of Moses or the writings of the prophets. No, I came to accomplish their purpose" (Matthew 5:17 NLT). Jesus came to fulfill and establish the proper meaning of the Torah, not to do away with the principles that God put in place for His people. Jesus provided the fullness and true meaning, the real thing instead of the type and shadow that existed under the Old Covenant.

The Early Church of New Testament believers recognized God's appointments with us as opportunities to honor God for what He has done in our lives—to appropriate the respective meanings and blessings. They serve as opportunities to celebrate who He is to us, and as a result of honoring God, today we can find great rewards for those who love and celebrate these divine appointments joyfully. This releases great blessings and benefits that God wants you to be able to receive! I pray your eyes are opened by revelation to receive all that He has for you!

The Fundamental Truths of Atonement

Let's linger just a moment to focus on what Jesus has done for us in the principle of the Day of Atonement. I mentioned before that it was a divine exchange. Though each of us has not committed every possible individual sin, we have all done one thing: we have all turned away from God to go our way, no matter what else we've done (see Isaiah 53:16). Accepting Jesus' offer of salvation is turning away from our path and receiving the gift of restitution with God.

At the cross, an exchange took place—all the evil due, by justice, to come to us, instead came upon Jesus. All of the good due to Jesus, earned by His sinless obedience, was made available to us.

Jesus was punished that we might be forgiven. He was wounded that we may be healed. He was made to be sin, covered with our sinfulness, that we could be made righteous, covered with His blood. Jesus died our death so that we may share His abundant life. He was cursed so that we could receive the blessing of the Father. He endured our poverty so that we could share His abundance. He bore our shame so that we could share His glory. Jesus took our rejection—remember that as He hung on the cross, He asked, "my God, my God, why have you forsaken me?"—so that we could accept His Sonship.

Our old man died in Jesus that His new Man might live in us. What an awesome God we serve, that He would release such an expression of measureless love to us, who were dead in our sins!

We are not required to follow the ancient blood sacrifices for our sins to be atoned, for Jesus settled all of that at the cross. However, we still celebrate and honor the principles and patterns, and the greatest of these was the atonement for our sins that Jesus paid for on the cross. I would say that is worthy of a feast!

It Is Finished!

Jesus' last words on the cross were, "It is finished!" This word, finished, means to do something perfectly. It could be translated "perfectly perfect." The atoning work of Jesus on the cross is perfect in every aspect and perfect in every respect.

We read in 2 Peter 1:3, "By his divine power, God has given us everything we need for living a godly life. We have received all of this by coming to know him, the one who called us to himself by means of his marvelous glory and excellence" (NLT).

Everything we will ever need was provided in that one sacrifice. Salvation is everything provided by the death of Jesus on the cross—rescue, deliverance, wholeness, healing, and eternal restoration with God.

On the Day of Atonement, we can honor Jesus and commemorate what He did for us. These feasts are more than just rituals or traditions; they are opportunities to encounter the Founder of the feasts in our hearts and preserve the principles He has eternally established.

He has a place at the feast for you—a reservation to meet him on the Mercy Seat on His Day of Atonement and honor Him for all that He has done for you. Will you keep it?

Chapter 12

Tabernacles

We have seen that God established all of Israel's worship to center on His feasts. They were occasions for celebration and enjoyment, but they were rich with meaning that we can appropriate for our lives today. The Fall Feasts started with Rosh Hashanah, the Feast of Trumpets, which was followed by ten days of reverential awe. These led to the holiest day, the Day of Atonement, and then five days later began the Feast of Tabernacles, which lasted for seven days. Let's talk about this, the Feast of Tabernacles—which I call "Party Time!"—because of all the feasts we're talking about in this section, this has some of the most fun and exciting promises for God's people. I'm going to frame it up for you in this chapter, and in the next one, I'm going to show you the very exciting principles God taught me about this feast.

This joyful seven-day festival contains many themes, but probably the heart of God can best be captured by the word "indwelling." God doesn't just want visitation rights—He wants habitation with you!

God lays out a lot of instructions in the book of Leviticus, including the specifics of this Feast of Tabernacles (which we could call the Feast of Booths or Shelters but was "Sukkot" to the Jews). In Leviticus 23, God explains the details of this festival.

The first day of the feast was a day of rest (as was the eighth day). God had them take the branches from the trees, palm fronds, those from leafy trees, and willows that grew by the streams, and create little shelters they would live in during the feast.

God tells them that this feast is to be a permanent law or ordinance for every generation to come (Leviticus 23:41), showing that this feast is an enduring principle the Lord does not want us to forget. Living outside in shelters that they built from tree branches was to remind them of how God had brought the Israelites out of Egypt.

After the seriousness of reverential awe and the Day of Atonement, the Feast of Tabernacles is a very joyful time. What I love most is that after the repentance and atonement came something very special: the unlimited blessings of restoration and all that God has promised His people!

In short, this feast was party time!

Yes, that's right—your God knows how to party, how to celebrate!

Season of Joy

God timed the Feast of Tabernacles to correspond to the fall grain harvest. It's a time of celebration for the blessing of the Lord, and the agricultural timing positioned it so that as the crops came in, the Israelites praised God for their provision for the year.

From a spiritual perspective, Feast of Tabernacles corresponds to the joy of knowing that our sins are forgiven. It also recalled God's miraculous provision and care after deliverance from bondage in Egypt (see Leviticus 23:43). Prophetically, Sukkot anticipates the coming of Jesus, where all the nations will come to Jerusalem to worship the Lord during the festival (see Zechariah

14:16). Because of Jesus' finished work, the price that He paid for us all as the High Priest of the New Covenant, we now have access to a Heavenly Temple (see Hebrews 4:16). We're now members of a greater Temple—the Body of Christ. Because of Jesus, Christians are part of His great Sukkot and can partake of all the blessings promised to God's people!

It's important to note when a pilgrimage feast comes around, the Lord impresses on us His enormous burden for the poor. The Lord was always reminding the Children of Israel to share with the poor from their abundance.

The reason we can have such joy, no matter our outside circumstances, is because we know the principles that God established for His people, and we can be a part of this blessing. While the Day of Atonement was the holiest day, in Biblical times Sukkot was considered the most important of all the Jewish holidays—they simply called it "the Feast." All of God's celebrations were important, but He specified that of all of them, this was the most important season.

God called for many sacrifices and offerings at this time, but it wasn't just a time where the people offered sacrifices—it's the season they were commanded to rejoice for the blessing of God's provision and care for their lives. As the harvest came in, they sacrificed as part of thanking God for their provision for the year, and God poured out His blessings on His people.

This was a season for praising God harder than they ever praised Him during the year. This was a season for blessing the Lord at all times, for recognizing how good He is above and beyond the normal.

And how did God tell them to commemorate this, the most important feast season on the calendar?

Have a party! Celebrate His goodness!

Party Time

During the Feast of Tabernacles, God's people had a continuous series of parties—as a family, together with friends, and before God. It was seven days of partying! What a God we serve who would command His people to part for seven days to celebrate His provision!

If you let it, this will change your view of God—for the better! This blows concepts of God as being a killjoy or anti-fun right out of the water. God was so pro-fun. He ordered His people to have parties and fun! Stop and just think about that for a moment, because this tells us so much about the character of God.

One of the best ways I've found to describe what "the Feast" is like is by telling people it's like seven days of Thanksgiving—a whole week of feasting, family, friends, rejoicing, giving thanks, and celebrating what we have to thank God for. It was a time for eating too much, fellowshipping into the night, enjoying one another's presence, and—most of all—remembering where all the goodness came from.

God provided, and now He told them to celebrate His provision.

Blessing Comes After Preparation

And after they had prepared their hearts before Him, He was getting ready to bust out all the stops:

> *"And it shall come to pass afterward that I will pour out My Spirit on all flesh; Your sons and your daughters shall prophesy, your old men shall dream dreams, your young men shall see visions. And also on My menservants and on My maidservants I will pour out*

My Spirit in those days" (Joel 2:28-29 NKJV).

This word "afterward" he uses referring to the time after the righteous preparation of Rosh Hashanah—after His people had prepared themselves with the Feast of Trumpets and the Day of Atonement. God made a time where His people prepared themselves to receive from Him, and as they went through the ten days of awe and the Day of Atonement, brought their best offerings, and honored God, they positioned themselves to receive God's protection, provision, and presence in the year to come.

Prophetically, we put ourselves in a position to receive the best from God when we let Him place our hearts as the Hebrews did in the Fall Feast Season. Obedience and a heart that is right toward God position you for a blessing. And the Feast of Tabernacles is all about the blessing!

Too many people encounter to expect to be blessed no matter what they do. They figure they can thumb their nose at God when things are going well but come running with their tail between their legs when they need Him. That is not honoring God, and though we receive His grace and forgiveness, that is not how we position ourselves to receive the blessing from the Lord.

The blessings of the Feast of Tabernacles came only after the Children of Israel had gone through a period of righteous preparation. They did more of the right things, let God adjust their hearts, repented, and sacrificed to position themselves so that God could bless them and they would still have the right attitude—honoring and giving God all the glory!

Everyone wants a blessing, but you cannot get the blessing without going through the processes God wants you to go through. God knows that your character needs to be able to handle your blessing. God loves you too much to leave you the same, so He is continually taking you from glory to glory—transforming you and conforming the character of Christ in you.

He knows your heart needs to be right so that the blessing does not instead become a curse.

With the way He arranged the Fall Feasts, God made it clear that you do not get a blessing without first making room in your heart for repentance. He established the principle that He blessed His people after the sacrifice—and notice that the sacrifice cost them something—and after they had been made right with Him on the Day of Atonement.

The blood of Jesus allows our hearts to be changed. We can intentionally focus on what it means for us and let what Jesus did sink in. Grasping the principles God established in these feasts for His people then will help us carry them over into our lives now and receive the same blessings He wants to give us, His people.

Let me make it clear that blessings are not simply "materialism." The greatest blessings are spiritual—your salvation and the work of the Holy Spirit. God's blessings can be relational, physical, emotional, and material.

Let God Prepare You

We must be ready to let God do whatever work He needs to do in our lives and in our hearts to prepare us for blessing. He has to bring us through hard things, knowing that they will shape us. Sometimes he has to cut off people who aren't right for us. He always has to get us over ourselves! We need to let go of whatever is holding us back from His best for us and from being who He desires us to be!

Our obedience brings us into an intimate encounter with the living God. These feasts are more than rituals or traditions; they are encounters with the Founder of the feasts and windows into His personality, desires, and principles.

God has an appointment waiting for you. He set it long ago. It's an appointment to bless you!

What he wants from you is that you will let Him do whatever He needs to position you to receive that blessing. He called the Children of Israel to ten days of reverential awe, repentance, sacrifice, and then the great feast that coincided with the harvest. Its purpose was that they celebrate all that He had done for them after they had prepared their hearts.

What has God done for you? What does He want you to remember and thank Him for that will position your heart to receive His best? As we look at these feasts, I hope you are grasping the timeless principles God sought to establish.

This chapter was just the preparation for the best part, because after we let Him prepare our hearts, then comes the blessing.

Take time and prepare your heart, just as the Children of Israel did before the Feast Tabernacles. Be open to whatever God may tell you. Be obedient to Him, and then get ready for the good part!

Are You Ready?

We have spent most of this section looking at how God prepared the hearts of His people so that they would be ready to receive His blessing. God knew that He first had to soften their hearts before He could bless them; otherwise, like the dry hard ground, the benefits would simply run off instead of soaking in.

In the Feast of Trumpets, God had His people look back at the year and soberly examine themselves. He had them look back to see all the ways they had missed the mark, and these ten days of reflection prepared them for repentance. This way, their hearts were ready for the Day of Atonement and the sacrifice that would cover over their sins.

But with their sins covered over and their hearts softened toward Him, God knew it was time for a party! But He didn't leave it with just feasting. Oh no, He had a lot more in store for them then just seven days of stuffing their faces, laughter, fellowship, and thanksgiving.

He has better plans for His kids than that!

Chapter 13

Party Time

There are eight promises found in the book of Joel that are expressions of God's favor for His people and come after the shofar sounds the Feast of Trumpets. These blessings are linked to the blessings God has for His people as they celebrate the harvest at the time of the Feast of Tabernacles. At this point in the Fall Feasts, God was ready to pour out His favor on His people!

God has demonstrated throughout Scripture that He delights in blessing His children. Some people hear about the idea of God's favor and think that it is unfair for Him to treat some people better than others. However, favor is actually very fair!

Favor has a pattern to it. It doesn't just happen; it's the result of obediently positioning yourself so that God can bless you. Favor comes as a result of allowing God to position you regarding righteousness, holiness, and obedience. It comes to those who fear the Lord and let Him make them wise. Favor is very fair because it's the result of letting obedience to God position your heart and life so that God can bless you!

The prophet Joel identified eight areas of favor with which God wants to bless His children. This favor took the form of restoration in the book of Joel; God was giving back to His people every blessing that they had missed, or that was taken from them.

The first blessing is increase—God wants to give a double

portion. Second, God wants to give His people revelation. Third, a fresh anointing. The fourth is God's power in the form of miracles. Next, God wants to minister restoration to His people. The sixth blessing is financial abundance. Seventh, God wants to replace shame with deliverance. And the eighth and final blessing is His presence.

The trumpet has sounded, you have honored God during His holy days, and now it's time to walk in the new day of the blessing of the Lord! Let's start with increase.

Increase

The word increase means to multiply, add, and reproduce—to make bigger or more. I bet that most of the people reading this wouldn't mind it if God wanted to bring increase to their lives!

The psalmist writes, "May the Lord give you increase more and more, You and your children" in Psalm 115:14. This principle of increase is all throughout the Word, but some people have limited it to the context of money. That isn't remotely the case! God wants to increase you in wisdom so you can make wise choices. He wants to increase your spiritual understanding so that you can comprehend the things of God. He wants to increase your capacity to handle His blessings and the call upon your life. He also wants to increase your gifts so that you can use them more effectively for the kingdom of God. Most importantly, He wants to increase His presence in your life—the role He plays in your everyday existence.

God wants to do all of this because He wants to make you more effective so that you can have a bigger impact on the lives of others. He wants the increase He gives to you to draw more people to Himself!

The prophet Joel writes, "Be glad then, you children of Zion, and rejoice in the Lord your God; for He has given you the former rain faithfully, and He will cause the rain to come down for you—the former rain, and the latter rain in the first month" (Joel 2:23 NKJV). He is referring to a type of increase we call a double portion.

You have to think like a farmer to understand this. With the rains come abundance, because this was a people connected to the land. When they got rains, they got harvests. Rains equal blessing to agricultural people, and to God (see Ezra 34:26).

The former rain, or early rain, Joel describes here are the spring rains, and they prepared the land for planting seed. The latter rains, or fall rains, prepared the land for harvest. The normal economy during the time of the prophet Joel would be that the former rains prepare the grain harvest in the latter rains prepare the fruit harvest, but what he is saying here is that God wants to give a double portion—the harvest of grain and fruit at the same time!

Now, what would happen if you received twice as much blessing—a double portion of rains—if your heart wasn't first prepared for it? Again, think agriculturally. If the people received twice as much rain all wants in the ground wasn't prepared, instead of a blessing they would have a flash flood!

Can you see how important it is to let God prepare your heart before you can receive blessing? You cannot handle a double portion blessing if you have not allowed God to prepare your heart beforehand. What should be a blessing will become a destructive flood if you are not ready to handle what God wants to give you!

Normally, we harvest after we have planted—that's the typical economy. However, the economy of increase is that God wants to bless you so abundantly that you're reaping at the same time you are sowing! This type of favor means there's no waiting in between; God wants to bless His people with a double portion and harvesting at the same time as they plant!

So, if there were something that would prevent you from receiving this harvest, would you want to know what it was? I certainly would! The answer to that is from Jeremiah. We read,

> *But my people have stubborn and rebellious hearts.*
> *They have turned away and abandoned me. They do*
> *not say from the heart, 'Let us live in awe of the Lord our*
> *God, for he gives us rain each spring and fall, assuring*
> *us of a harvest when the time is right.' Your wickedness*
> *has deprived you of these wonderful blessings. Your sin*
> *has robbed you of all these good things.*
> *(Jeremiah 5:23-25 NLT)*

So what prevents us from receiving this former and latter rain at the same time, this double portion?

It's when we do not recognize God as the Giver. Every good thing comes from God. Our defiant and rebellious hearts and our sin rob us of the increase God wants to give us, and this principle stands true for each of the other blessings I'm about to share with you—rebellion and sin will rob you of them.

God does not want us ever to lack in any area of our lives. However, it's up to us as His people to prepare our lives, to repent, to increase our capacity to receive God's abiding and abundant grace and blessings. Learn from the principle of the Fall Feasts, and let God prepare your heart for a double portion!

Revelation

In Joel 2:24 he prophecies that our threshing floors would be full of wheat. Wheat represents revelation in the Bible, and we can all use more revelation, as most of us don't have threshing floors anymore!

Revelation is a key blessing God promises to His people. Revelation is a special or extraordinary manifestation that removes the veil from something—it reveals things to us so that we can understand them. Revelation is receiving God's insight into situations so that we can perceive and understand what He's doing—and what we should be doing.

King David, the psalmist, prayed, "Open my eyes to see the wonderful truths in your instructions" (Psalm 119:18). Paul echoes this when he writes that he prays, "that the God of our Lord Jesus Christ, the Father of glory, may give to you the spirit of wisdom and revelation in the knowledge of Him, the eyes of your understanding being enlightened." Paul is asking that they "may know what is the hope of His calling, what are the riches of the glory of His inheritance in the saints, and what is the exceeding greatness of His power toward us who believe, according to the working of His mighty power" (Ephesians 1:17-19 NKJV).

This is revelation and what it does for us. It lets us perceive God's power that's at work in us—the same mighty power that raised Christ from the dead and seated Him in the place of honor at God's right hand (see Ephesians 1:20). This will be essential for a later blessing, as we'll see: we need revelation of God's power because He promises we will operate in His power!

Revelation is based on how God wants us to see things. In short, He wants us to have His perspective. Again, this is why we must allow Him to position our hearts; we need to receive His perspective. When we have His perspective, we see things with His eyes—and we will grow in our spiritual wisdom and knowledge of God, flooding our hearts with hope and light. The hope is in Him—and in the inheritance, He gives to us, His people.

Fresh Anointing & Power

Joel goes on in 2:24 to prophecy that "the vats shall overflow with new wine and oil" (NKJV). The wine vats that he refers to here were excavated troughs of a winepress. The winepress is a biblical picture of overflowing, abundant joy or a fresh anointing. It's God's power at work in your life!

The New Testament fulfillment of this is found in John 10:10 when Jesus says of Himself, "I have come that they may have life, and that they may have it more abundantly" (NKJV).

When we are anointed, we're endowed by God to function in a particular capacity. It's blessing for a purpose. Whenever God anoints people, it's because He intends them to do something! It wasn't for them; it was for His purpose.

Samuel anointed David to become king of Israel by pouring out oil over his head. It ran through his hair and streamed down around his ears, his eyes, and flowed in rivulets down his neck— it covered his whole head. But it wasn't a force field against adversity; it prepared David for God's work. David proceeded to wait for years before the people recognized him as their king, and all the while he was dodging spears from Saul, Philistine swords, and the threat of betrayal.

Through it all, God was with David, and he was anointed to do God's work. He excelled at everything he did, and he received God's blessing. When presented with the opportunity to take matters into his hands and make himself king by killing Saul, David preserved the Lord's anointing by restraining himself and not sinning. Instead, he just kept doing God's work, and eventually his circumstances caught up with his anointing when he was made the king of Israel.

Your anointing has a purpose, and that purpose is to function in a capacity that you otherwise could not do without God's empowerment.

God's Power

The oil also symbolizes the power of God for miracles. God has always performed signs and wonders on behalf of His people, and He almost always used a human vessel to do His mighty work.

Jeremiah writes, "You have brought Your people Israel out of the land of Egypt with signs and wonders, with a strong hand and an outstretched arm, and with great terror" (Jeremiah 32:21 NKJV). God's chosen vessel? A stuttering murderer named Moses whom God had to talk into obeying Him. Your past does not determine your future.

Daniel writes, "How great are His signs, and how mighty His wonders! His kingdom is an everlasting kingdom, and His dominion is from generation to generation" (Daniel 4:3 NKJV). Daniel, an exiled Jew living in Babylon, later experienced this firsthand when God delivered him from the mouths of hungry lions.

C.S Lewis defines miracles as "an interference with nature by supernatural power," and they have a way of settling issues. Jesus' miracles created the separation between those who received Him and those who rejected Him. Everywhere He went, miracles followed—the blind could see, the deaf could hear, and even the dead rising again. These miracles drew some people to Him, but they seemed to push others (the Pharisees) away.

Now, get ready for the shocker: Jesus said that as many mighty miracles as He did, we would do more! He told us, "Most assuredly, I say to you, he who believes in Me, the works that I do he will do also; and greater works than these he will do, because

I go to My Father" (John 14:12 NKJV). God will use you to bring glory to Himself—so that others may believe.

Be ready, because God wants to give you His favor with miracles of provision, healing, protection, wisdom, and more! God is willing to superimpose His invisible kingdom over the laws of nature, and He wants to bless you with His power to experience miracles in your daily life.

Restoration

We often say that time is the one thing we cannot get back. But the prophet Joel goes on to say, "So I will restore to you the years that the swarming locust has eaten" (Joel 2:25 NKJV). God will restore the years to you!

The word "restore" here is shalam, which is a verb similar to the noun shalom, the Hebrew word for peace. Locusts often represent demons or satanic minions in the Bible; they are a thieving force of nature when they sweep in and devour a crop, and their nature is similar to how the enemy seeks to devour good things in our lives.

God here promises to restore you back to your original condition—before corruption and before loss. Before the devil, the thief, stole and destroyed in your life. God promises to restore what the devil has stolen! You see, nothing is lost when you serve God. You must ask God for revelation so you can see from His perspective. Remember, God's ways are not man's ways, and His thoughts are higher than ours (see Isaiah 55:9).

Jesus promised,

> *Assuredly, I say to you, there is no one who has left*
> *house or brothers or sisters or father or mother or wife*
> *or children or lands, for My sake and the gospel's, who*

shall not receive a hundredfold now in this time—
houses and brothers and sisters and mothers and
children and lands, with persecutions—and in the age
to come, eternal life.
(Matthew 10:29-30 NKJV)

We see examples of God restoring what was lost in the story of Job. The devil was given permission to steal from Job, and he took from him every good thing—but he could not take away his commitment to obeying God. Job has an incredible encounter with God, where he brought his questions to God…and received an answer like none other! And in the end, God restored to Job much, much more than the devil had stolen. And you know that on the other side of his trial, Job's walk with God was stronger than ever before.

Supernatural restoration is a process that begins in our Savior. As your life is filled with God's Word, and you act upon God's faith, you will have authority to take back or regain what has been stolen from you! God will restore that which has been stolen.

Financial Abundance

"You shall eat in plenty and be satisfied, and praise the name of the Lord your God, who has dealt wondrously with you," Joel goes on (Joel 2:26 NKJV). This is a direct contrast to the previous report of famine (see Joel 1:4,20,29), and it is a promise from God to provide abundantly for His people.

This is different than increase, because while increase can be in nearly any category, providing abundantly for our daily needs is God's promise always to take care of His people with provision specifically. This promise is tied closely to the timing of the Feast of Tabernacles, which coincides with the fall harvest to help remind God's people that He is their provider.

David writes in Psalms 23, "You prepare a feast for me in the presence of my enemies. You honor me by anointing my head with oil. My cup overflows with blessings" (v.5 NLT). God provides a feast at His banqueting table—and His table is full of blessings.

Here again, we see how important our hearts are. God yearns to bless His people materially, but He first has to prepare our hearts. God's blessings have to do with so much more than just financial gain, as I told you earlier, but before He can bless you in this way, He must first purify your motives.

If your motive for wanting to tap into His blessings is merely to accumulate riches, you won't triumph but will instead bring pain and suffering to yourself. The wisest man who ever lived writes, "A life devoted to things is a dead life, a stump; a God-shaped life is a flourishing tree" (Proverbs 11:28 MSG).

While there are many places where the Word tells us God desires to bless us, it is also full of warnings that if we put our trust in riches, we will fall. Those who place their faith in money may eventually lose both their "faith" and their finances because they've let riches supplant God. Remember, God looks at the heart, and He can tell when your heart is prepared for a double-portion of blessing—and when it's not.

Being ready for God to bless you materially starts with firmly acknowledging that God is your source. In the gospels, Jesus recognizes God as His source 176 times. Our Father owns the cattle on a thousand hills—all cattle on every hill, really—and He loves to provide for His children.

Think back to the importance of firstfruits—of acknowledging God first. One of the worst mistakes we can make—spiritually, emotionally, physically, and especially financially is to depend on our strength and knowledge and ignore God's proper position as First.

We must remember, no matter how much He gives us, we are only stewards. We are temporary caretakers of God's earthly possessions; they're on loan from God. And to those who show they are trustworthy with little, He will entrust even more. But when we demonstrate that our motives are selfish and worldly, we show that our hearts aren't ready for this kind of blessing.

Only when we do it God's way, in obedience, does God trust us enough to bless us with a double portion of finances. Prosperity isn't the result of pursuing wealth; it comes from obedience.

I could quote so many verses to you here—that God is the one who gives us the ability to gain wealth (Isaiah 48:17), that the love of money is the root of all evil (1 Timothy 6:10), and so much more, but what I want you to grasp most is this: when we seek Him first, God adds all the rest to us in time.

In 2 Chronicles 26:5 we read a piece of the story of the boy king Uzziah and get a quote for the concept I most want you to take away from this promise of prosperity: "as long as he sought the Lord, God made him prosper" (NKJV).

Deliverance Instead of Shame

If you have failed in life, ever, you deal with shame. So did God's people, and that is why Joel writes, "Then you shall know that I am in the midst of Israel: I am the Lord your God and there is no other. My people shall never be put to shame. And it shall come to pass that whoever calls on the name of the Lord shall be saved" (Joel 2:27,32 NKJV).

In Ephesians chapter 6, Paul points out that we are engaged in a spiritual battle with the kingdom of darkness. One of the enemy's choice weapons is shame—he reminds us of everything we've done wrong, every time we've failed, and all the ways we're not qualified or are disqualified by our failures. The Word calls him the accuser of the brethren, and he's superb at it.

However, we have God's answer to the accuser: "No weapon formed against you shall prosper, and every tongue which rises against you in judgment you shall condemn. This is the heritage of the servants of the Lord, and their righteousness is from Me" (Isaiah 54:17 NKJV).

The reality is that the battle has been won already! Jesus defeated the enemy, and we don't need to fight for our victory because we walk in victory! The battle is won! Victory is ours, and we live it by taking our authority over the voice of the enemy that seeks to shame us. We are saved—blood-bought children of God.

End of story.

God's Presence

And now back to my favorite verse in this passage from Joel: "And it shall come to pass afterward that I will pour out My Spirit on all flesh; your sons and your daughters shall prophesy, your old men shall dream dreams, your young men shall see visions. And also on My menservants and on My maidservants I will pour out My Spirit in those days" (Joel 2:28-29 NKJV).

"Those days" are now! God's Sprit has already been poured out; He poured it freely on Pentecost, and now every human being can be restored to relationship with God through Jesus Christ and receive His Spirit! No longer does the Holy Spirit rest temporarily on God's people—He can fall on all of us at the same time.

God's presence is promised, and delivered, to you. He is with you wherever you go, whatever you do. And He who is in you is doing a restorative work from the inside out, transforming you into the image of His Son. God's presence brings real transformation—not us just "acting like" Christians, but the Spirit-powered ability to live a godly life.

Every promise, every principle, and every hope that God established in His feasts are wrapped up in Jesus Christ. When He lives within us, we have the very power that raised Christ from the dead at work within us. We have the Holy Spirit with us to teach us all things! As we celebrate the feasts, these divine appointments, voluntarily and out of a joyful and obedient heart, we will reap great rewards.

I pray you're catching this: these feasts are more than a ritual, more than a tradition. When we experience them, we encounter the Founder of the feasts in our hearts as well as our intellects. These divine appointments offer us timeless opportunities to focus in on the magnificent Lord, who created these feasts and showed portions of Himself to His people through them.

So what is He showing you?

Chapter 14

The Spirit Poured Out

Fifty days after Passover came the feast of Pentecost. It was the extravagant culmination of the harvesting season of grain. From the day that the set-apart barley sheaves were waved before the Lord, the Israelites were to count off seven weeks. These forty-nine days brought them to the wheat harvest, the more nourishing and valued grain. This festival has to do with Revelation and harvest.

The Lord specified that the people should give a free will offering in proportion to the blessings the Lord had given each one. This was a joyful festival of provision and harvest.

Luke reports, "And they worshiped Him, and returned to Jerusalem with great joy, and were continually in the temple praising and blessing God" (Luke 24:52-53). One hundred and twenty of them remained in prayer until the Feast of Weeks (Pentecost) arrived, and when it did, they were gathered together, as we'll talk about later (see Acts 1:14-15, 2:1).

I've saved Pentecost for the end because while most of the other feasts were about preparation, atonement, and blessing, this was the empowerment that enabled the early believers actually to do God's work on the earth. What happened on the Day of Pentecost after Jesus was raised from the dead was the fulfillment of promises from the Old Testament, especially the promise from

Joel that God was going to pour out His Spirit upon all flesh.

But He didn't do this just for fun or for their edification; He did it to prepare them for the harvest. And He is still giving His Holy Spirit for that reason—to bless us, yes, but to empower the workers in the harvest so that He can draw all men to Himself.

The Day of Pentecost

God set a divine appointment with His people hundreds of years in advance—not just the feast of Pentecost, but the singular "Day of Pentecost" where the Holy Spirit descended upon those gathered in the upper room. We read the account of this in Acts:

When the Day of Pentecost had fully come, they were all with one accord in one place. And suddenly there came a sound from heaven, as of a rushing mighty wind, and it filled the whole house where they were sitting. Then there appeared to them divided tongues, as of fire, and one sat upon each of them. And they were all filled with the Holy Spirit and began to speak with other tongues, as the Spirit gave them utterance.

(Acts 2:1-4 NKJV)

Peter then gives us the spiritual context of what happened as he says,

But this is what was spoken by the prophet Joel: 'And it shall come to pass in the last days, says God, that I will pour out of My Spirit on all flesh; your sons and your daughters shall prophesy, your young men shall see visions, your old men shall dream dreams. And on My menservants and on My maidservants I will pour out My Spirit in those days; and they shall prophesy.

(Acts 2:16-18 NKJV)

The Day of Pentecost happened there in Acts, but just like all these feasts, we still celebrate the principles today—and we still experience the empowerment today! I want us to spend our time talking about Pentecost looking at a few important things, starting with the preparation and relationship that's the vital foundation for walking in the Holy Spirit. God gives us His power—dunamis—which descended on the believers in the upper room. This empowerment was not limited to those gathered in the upper room only weeks after Jesus' ascension into heaven, but the Holy Spirit isn't just about the working of miracles—He's about relationship.

The power that fell on them continues to fall on believers who are open to the indwelling presence of the Holy Spirit, the third Person of the Trinity. The power they received is just waiting to be released in an intimate relationship we can all have with God the Holy Spirit.

But all too often, Christians are either frightened of the Holy Spirit because they've heard false teaching, or they're preoccupied with seeking power, gifts, and moves of the Spirit. Together, we're going to see that God has a plan for how He pours out His Spirit—and like all His plans, it's perfect.

The Person of Pentecost

Many people treat the Holy Spirit as though He's this mystical "force," an unpredictable spiritual energy that defies our understanding and is somehow less trustworthy and acceptable than God the Son and God the Father. Incorrect teaching within parts of the Church has cast the Holy Spirit into a negative light that the third Person of the Trinity does not deserve, and everyone who has received this teaching and has rejected or mistrusted the Holy Spirit is missing out on incredible blessing and power that God wishes us to experience.

The Holy Spirit is as much God—as trustworthy and worthy of our honor and reverence—as the Father and the Son, and He is a Person that we can know intimately and personally. His Person is the evidence of His presence in our lives, and together we're going to look at what God intended for Pentecost, how it was fulfilled on the Day of Pentecost, and how that empowerment has not gone out of style but is available to enrich the life of every believer.

I want to start our talk of the Holy Spirit (the gift we received on the Day of Pentecost) with one of the most important verses about Him in all of Scripture. Jesus is speaking, and He tells us, "It is to your advantage that I go away; for if I do not go away, the Helper will not come to you; but if I depart, I will send Him to you" (John 16:7 NKJV).

We're going to get back to this, but let's quickly look at another statement Jesus made, this one from Acts: "But you shall receive power when the Holy Spirit has come upon you; and you shall be witnesses to Me in Jerusalem, and in all Judea and Samaria, and to the end of the earth" (Acts 1:8 NKJV).

Let's just linger here with these Scriptures for one moment. Have you ever thought, consciously or subconsciously, that if only Jesus would show up in your living room and wave His hand over your life, everything would be okay? I know of people who think this way—that all they needed was for Him to appear and touch their situation as He did in the Gospels and it would all work out.

But in the very words of Jesus Himself, He tells us that it's better for us that He went away!

Stop and think about this for a moment: the Helper Jesus sent is so good, He is better than having the physical Jesus on the earth. Have you ever really grasped that idea? Have you ever let that sink into your spirit—that we have something better now than when Jesus walked the earth?

And the next passage tells us why: because when the Holy Spirit came, He gave believers access to His power—His dunamis—to do God's will on the earth. This power, this dunamis, is a power that's capable of reproducing itself; it's power to spread the Good News across the whole earth. We get our word "dynamite" from this word because it is explosive power to do God's will—not for our gratification but to bring God glory.

Jesus, as impossibly amazing and beautiful as the Son of God given flesh was, was fully God...but also fully man. He was limited to one place in space and time, just like us. The Man, Jesus Christ, could not be with every single one of us all the time.

But that's not true of the Holy Spirit—the Spirit is everywhere, all at once, doing God's will and empowering believers with the dunamis to work God's will all over this planet. He is within us, and we can all experience His power.

This power is what enables believers to lay their hands on the sick and see them recover. It's what allows you to speak out a revelation or a prophetic word or a word of knowledge and see it change people's lives. It's what lets us walk in faith and change the world and bring God the glory!

Now, think on this: did the believers before the Day of Pentecost have Jesus in their hearts? Had they believed in Him? Yes! But Jesus Himself told them, "Do not leave Jerusalem until the Father sends you the gift he promised, as I said before. John baptized with water, but in just a few days you will be baptized with the Holy Spirit" (Acts 1:4-5 NLT).

If the first believers had everything they needed, why did Jesus tell them to wait to receive another gift from the Father? They needed power!

If this promise of the Holy Spirit and His power was so important and significant that Jesus Himself tells us it's better for us that He go away so the Helper can come, wouldn't you say that it's important for us to know who He is and what His role is in the life of believers? I'd say it's critical, so let's learn more about Him together.

The Holy Spirit Is A Gentleman

The first aspect of the Holy Spirit that I want you to know is that He never plays the role of a dictator in the life of a believer. The Holy Spirit never forces His way into a life, and He doesn't force believers to do things as though He were manipulating a puppet.

I can't tell you how many people I've talked to who are afraid that if they're open to the Holy Spirit that He'll make them do crazy things; that He'll violate their control of their bodies or something. This belief is simply foolish superstition, and nothing could be further from the truth.

It has been rightly said that the Holy Spirit is a Gentleman— He doesn't force Himself on anyone. He offers His empowerment to witness and do God's will to every Christian, but He doesn't force it on anyone. Don't be afraid that the Holy Spirit is going to make you do things against your will; that's not scriptural.

What is scriptural is that He desires to be closer than a brother—to be our Helper, our Advocate, and our Counselor. Each of these relationships requires intimacy.

Hunger for Intimacy

Everything that the Holy Spirit does in our lives flows out of an intimate relationship with us. Every fruit that He produces in the life of the believer is a result of who He is, and this is another source of problems I see regarding believers and the Holy Spirit. Too often, I see people who are after the results of what He does, but they're disinterested in who He is.

The Holy Spirit is not a force we direct or control like we're on Star Wars. He is a Person whom we intimately encounter as part of a deepening walk with God.

If you are saved and hungering more for God, it is the Holy Spirit that you're yearning for! Hunger for God shifts your atmosphere; it drives you to seek more of Him, to dive deeper. And when you go deeper, the Holy Spirit is who you'll find.

If you are hungry for more of God, you must welcome the Holy Spirit into your life, because He is a Gentleman, and He will not force Himself upon you. You have to seek Him, welcome Him.

But I want to give you some good news—you don't have to be anywhere special or get help from anyone to receive the Holy Spirit. You can welcome Him into your life at any stage of your Christian walk, and you will go from a believer who's accepted Jesus and been transformed into a new creature into a powerhouse of God, radically supercharged with the dunamis of the Holy Spirit!

So remember what I said: you must understand who the Holy Spirit is to understand what He can do in your life. So as we look at what God set up with Pentecost and what He fulfilled at the Day of Pentecost when He sent the Holy Spirit, we're going to learn more about who the Holy Spirit is so you can welcome more of His power into your life. So let's learn some more together!

Chapter 15

Hello— My Name is the Holy Spirit

As we learn more about who the Holy Spirit is, we can look for no better source than Jesus Himself to tell us about His Spirit. When Jesus spoke to His disciples about the Holy Spirit, He used words like Helper, Comforter, Guide, and Teacher to describe Him.

Jesus also told us that the Holy Spirit was in proper alignment with God's order—that He doesn't say anything on His own, but only what Jesus shows Him. John 16:13-14 says, "However, when He, the Spirit of truth, has come, He will guide you into all truth; for He will not speak on His own authority, but whatever He hears He will speak; and He will tell you things to come. He will glorify Me, for He will take of what is Mine and declare it to you."

The Holy Spirit always stays within the roles that He's ascribed by Jesus. He doesn't ever compel a believer to do anything, and He does nothing that He has not received from Jesus.

So let me propose this to anyone who has ever been "afraid" of what the Holy Spirit would do if He had free reign in your life: Do you trust Jesus? Many who doubt the Holy Spirit trust Jesus, so how can they read the Scripture above, which explicitly says that the Spirit speaks exactly that which He hears from Jesus, and then doubt the work of the Holy Spirit? It just doesn't make sense.

Any doubts and fears about the Spirit are not the results of His true move on the earth—it's the result of incorrect teaching.

So who is the Holy Spirit? Here are some aspects I have pulled from Scripture about Him: He is God. He's the divine power of God and God's creative Spirit. He is the Spirit of Truth, the Spirit of might and power, the Spirit of counsel, the Spirit of wisdom and understanding, the Spirit of glory, and the Spirit of Christ. Helper, Comforter, Guide, and Teacher. He's omnipresent (everywhere present), He's omniscient (all knowing), and He's omnipotent (all powerful).

Let those things soak in for a moment; read over them again. Get them inside your heart—this is who the Holy Spirit is. Is anything in there frightening or doubtful?

What about this one—He is God? He's co-equal, part of the Trinity. He's not the lesser branch of the Godhead. He isn't a consolation prize for losing Jesus' presence on the earth. He's better than having a physical Jesus!

We do not grow in our walk with Christ or power as believers by wanting what He does in our lives; we grow by knowing who He is by knowing Him intimately. We grow by welcoming Him into our lives, by making room for Him, and by letting our hunger for more of God drive us to a deeper relationship with the Holy Spirit.

The Person of the Holy Spirit

It's important to know that the Holy Spirit is not some mystical figment of our imagination, an old part of the Trinity who's day passed on Pentecost or during the age of the Early Church, or a superstitious spiritual force. He's not a ghost, and He's not a possessing Spirit that violates the will of the believer. He's not an "it."

He is a Person—and He's God.

And like any person, He has a mind, will, and emotions. He loves, and He grieves, and we can get to know Him on an intimate personal level.

Not too many people think about the Holy Spirit having feelings, but like any individual we can get to know, He has emotions. You can grieve the Holy Spirit, through sin. You can excite Him, as you grasp and understand more about Him and welcome more of His power into your life so that the power of God can move on the earth through you.

The Holy Spirit has a job to do—He carries on the work of Christ in and through us. But again, we must understand who He is before we can understand what He does.

I want your emphasis to be on wanting to know the Holy Spirit as a Person just as much as you do Jesus, but I also want to give you a biblical context for what He does, because He has a purpose. Here are some of his roles as related to the Word.

The Holy Spirit gives us the mind of Christ. He speaks the mind of God, teaches the will of God, and witnesses the things of God. He is the revealer of the wisdom of God, and He brings inward illumination. He guides the people of God, convicts us of sin so we'll repent, and helps us. He indwells us, regenerates us, seals us in Christ, and guarantees our inheritance. He baptizes us in Himself, fills us with God's power, and performs miracles. He reaches out to sinners, revealing their sin to them.

Remember, the presence of the Holy Spirit is evidence that the Person of the Holy Spirit is here—you don't get His fruit, His evidence, if you do not know Him as a Person. I often hear people who say they want the anointing, but the anointing is simply the manifested presence of God. So how do we experience this manifested presence of God? We get to know the Holy Spirit better as a Person.

Chase the Person, Not the Manifestation

Instead of chasing after the anointing, we ought to pursue after knowing the Person of the Holy Spirit better. As you pursue the presence of God and His Spirit, His presence will manifest in the form of the anointing.

I mentioned people who seem afraid of the Holy Spirit, but now I want to address those who know they're Spirit-filled: we aren't to chase after the moves of God, we're to chase after God. We're not after His evidence because the evidence will come as we know the Person better!

You do not need a service or gathering to experience the presence of the Holy Spirit. While we participate with God corporately as a Body, His movement isn't limited to that, and we get to know Him intimately during our one-on-one, face-to-face times. Your times of intimate communion are what will help you know the Holy Spirit better, not chasing after events where His presence is falling. One of the greatest errors is first trying to know the work of the Holy Spirit before you first come to know the Holy Spirit Himself!

Again, the Holy Spirit is a Person, and you'll get to know Him in a personal setting.

Often, Spirit-filled believers seem to be chasing the manifestation, but they fail to realize that the Spirit makes His dwelling within born-again believers. Paul writes, "Do you not know that you are the temple of God and that the Spirit of God dwells in you?" (1 Corinthians 3:16)

The Holy Spirit is omnipresent, and He lives in each of us. This is why we can say that greater is He that is in me that he that's in the world!

Think on this: the Holy Spirit isn't in the church—the building.

He's in us! We are His temple! We are just jars of clay, but the very power that raised Christ from the dead lives within us.

More Real

If you have ever felt uncomfortable in your skin, like you never quite fit, like a square peg in a round hole, it's because we all have a longing within us for what is real—the spiritual. But we can easily get trapped into paying attention solely to the physical.

Though we typically can't see it with our eyes, the spiritual world is more real than this physical one. The Spirit within you is the resource that allows you to tap into the spiritual world of greater reality where God operates. It's what allows you to put off the sinful nature, with its addiction and negativity and lust and anger and everything else, and instead put on the incorruptible, the righteous, and the dunamis power of God.

Whatever problems you may have, from relationships to health to provision to behavioral to emotional wounds and hurts, you can tap into the eternal you—the spirit you—through an intimate relationship with the Holy Spirit. His Spirit speaks to our spirit, and the Holy Spirit can do the work on the inside of us that we can never do to ourselves.

We don't fix ourselves from the outside in—by trying to change our behavior. We experience genuine and lasting change when the Holy Spirit transforms us from the inside out!

Our behavior always stems from our beliefs. So what are you believing? Do you think it's your job to change you? Or have you realized yet that it's the Holy Spirit that will transform you by the renewing of your mind?

The Holy Spirit is not the movement or the manifestation. He's not a ritual or doing the right things so that God will bless you and infill you more. You don't get more of Him by attending church more often, saying certain Bible verses like they're incantations, or trying harder to do things right.

We experience His work in our lives as we spend time with Him, getting to know Him and what He likes and dislikes. One of the surest ways to block the changes the Holy Spirit wants to make in your life is by grieving Him.

Pleasing the Spirit

Paul cautions the Ephesian believers, "And do not grieve the Holy Spirit of God, by whom you were sealed for the day of redemption" (Ephesians 4:30). Another translation puts it like this: "Don't grieve God. Don't break his heart. His Holy Spirit, moving and breathing in you, is the most intimate part of your life, making you fit for himself. Don't take such a gift for granted" (MSG).

The Holy Spirit is a Person, and like any other person, there are things we can do that hurt Him or grieve Him, as well as things that excite Him and bring Him joy.

When I was about nineteen or twenty, I prayed all night one time and asked God to give me His heart. The next morning, I went to a restaurant, and I can still clearly remember seeing the waitress as she came up to take my order. When I looked in her eyes, it wasn't the same as I'd seen people the day before. I saw her through the heart of God, and I wasn't seeing her from the outside; I was seeing her as God saw her, from the inside. My chest was pounding, and I felt like it was the very heartbeat of God for His people surging within me, trying to beat out of my chest!

I was excited by the Holy Spirit, and the longing I felt for this waitress to know God wasn't my own—it was the Holy Spirit's. It was exhilarating! It's the highest of highs because it springs up from our spirits as we draw near to God's Spirit. I'm an analytical person, but I have learned that there's nothing to compare to jumping in and yielding to the Holy Spirit because He changes and transforms us from the inside out.

Pleasing the Holy Spirit is an out of this world encounter because it's part of God's invisible world of Spirit that we can only experience through the Holy Spirit.

We can so easily become distracted and think that the Christian life is all about our behavior. We try to fix things—to fix ourselves—by changing the way we act and by trying to get our behavior to conform to what we think a good Christian should be like. But this isn't the path to true change! We experience true change when we are pleasing the Holy Spirit and can feel Him making us more like Christ.

The Holy Spirit wants to be closer to you than a brother—closer than your best friend, closer than your parents, closer even than your spouse. And you'll find that as you pursue a relationship with the Him, you will conclude that the Spirit will always take you closer to Jesus first, and Jesus will get you to the Father.

The Spirit, as we've said before, doesn't force Himself on anyone. So if we're hungry for more of God, we must pursue intimately knowing Him. We don't come to the Holy Spirit demanding His move and results in our lives; we draw near to Him, and He shows us the path to the heart of God (through His Son).

Our hunger brings us to the Spirit, and the results of knowing Him better include being satisfied with more and more and more of God's transforming presence in our lives. He will show us who you are in covenant, your identity through Jesus Christ and that you now have the same DNA as our "older Brother," Jesus. He's going to show you who your adoptive Daddy is so that you can know Him intimately as Abba Father.

God the Spirit takes us to God the Son, who leads us to God the Father. But He only does so in relationship. You won't be drawn to God the Father through ritual, by rule-keeping, or by trying to follow the manifestations of the Spirit. You will be drawn from Spirit to Son, to Father.

Want to see the power and work of the Holy Spirit manifesting in your life? Great! Get to know Him. Forget the results of knowing Him and just focus on Him.

Because when you intimately know the Person of the Holy Spirit, the fruit will follow. With that firmly established, now we can look at His fruit in our lives—because, believe me, you want this kind of fruit in your life!

Chapter 16

Your Fruit Will Prove Your Relationship

In the previous chapters, we started our final feast, Pentecost, by talking about the Holy Spirit. I've been focusing on Him because Pentecost is really about your relationship with the Holy Spirit. Pentecost was the fulfillment of God's promise through the prophet Joel that He would pour out His Spirit upon all people, and on the Day of Pentecost, the believers assembled in the upper room received God's power—His dunamis—to do His work throughout the earth.

To remove the confusion that's so prevalent in the Church about the Holy Spirit, I've wanted to impress the importance of intimately knowing Him as a Person. While some have grown up under teaching that makes them doubt or even fear the Holy Spirit, many others seem only interested in what He can give them—what they can get out of being near His moves.

The reality is that the Holy Spirit is the third Person of the Trinity—He's just as much God as Jesus, and the Father are—and that no one can come to Jesus without the Holy Spirit. He passes on to us everything we need for life and godliness—but only that which He receives from Jesus. So if we trust Jesus, we must trust His Spirit.

But we don't grow in intimacy with the Holy Spirit by simply learning about Him or being near His moves; we get to know Him personally when we open ourselves and invest in a relationship.

With our focus on Him as a Person, on our relationship and not on what we can get out of it, we're ready to cover what He does in more detail. The function of the Holy Spirit in the life of the believer is nothing short of miraculous. He's the energy source, the power, the dunamis that makes the Christian life possible— but not just possible, victorious and infectious! He was sent to comfort us, to help us, to counsel us, to teach us all things—but He was also sent to empower Christians to spread the Good News about Jesus to every corner of the earth and every lost and hurting person on this planet.

His Fruit Reveals His Character

While we don't go seeking the gifts of the Spirit and His fruit for their sake—we receive those as part of knowing Him better— He is impossible to separate from the blessings He gives us. The fruit of the Spirit is the proof of relationship with Him, not His gifts. Let me explain what I mean by that.

I have met people who put their emphasis on the gifts the Holy Spirit gives us and others who emphasize the fruit, the truth is that the Bible treats them equally. But let me say this—I have met people who appear to have the gifts of the Spirit but who were lacking the fruit of the spirit. More than His gifts, His fruit is the evidence that someone has an intimate relationship with the Person of the Holy Spirit.

Paul writes, "But the fruit of the Spirit is love, joy, peace, longsuffering, kindness, goodness, faithfulness, gentleness, self-control" (Galatians 5:22-23). You probably don't have to think hard to bring to mind a Christian you've met who seems totally lacking these fruit in their lives! We all have—we've met un-loving, unhappy, frantic, fragile, rude, self-seeking, back-biting, and impulsive so-called Christians.

The power of His gifts descended on the Day of Pentecost; they didn't have to wait long to receive those. And when it comes to it, God can do mighty works even through a donkey if He chooses—He can use anyone, no matter how rough around the edges. A person can get saved, and the same night they may prophesy. But I doubt that a person could get saved and operate in the maturity or fruit that the Spirit brings, simply because they have not spent time walking with Him and getting to know Him.

I believe that when we do not show the fruit of the Spirit in our lives, it illustrates we need a deeper personal relationship with the Person of the Holy Spirit. We all have our off days, and we all struggle with sin; this isn't just about our behavior. But when we put our emphasis on what the Holy Spirit does instead of His character taking root in us, our lives will become out of alignment. We may walk in the gifts of the Spirit, but if we do not have the fruit of the Spirit, we are not showing maturity in Christ.

The Holy Spirit imparts the character of God to us through relationship with Him. So let's look at the aspects of His character that Paul calls out.

Love—God is love. It's who He is! This is divine love that God has for us—a strong, ardent, tender, compassionate love that isn't self-seeking and gives us what we need the most even when we deserve it the least. This love is unconditional agape love that flows out of us, thanks to being close to the Spirit.

Joy, it's important to note, is different than happiness. Happiness is dictated by circumstances, but the joy of the Spirit is emotional gladness, delight, and excitement that transcends your circumstances and instead finds its power source in God. It's delight over blessings you've received, expect to receive, or that you're excited about for others.

Peace isn't the absence of conflict; it's the state of emotional quietness, rest, repose, harmony, order, and security we can experience through God despite the turmoil, strife, and temptation. You can have peace right in the middle of your stuff—and believe me when people see this, it's a tremendous testimony to the power of God at work in your life.

The Spirit gives us peace that passes our understanding. During one of the most difficult seasons of my life, I can remember thinking that I wasn't going to make it through. While laying on the floor, I felt like I simply could not pick myself up. And the reality was that in myself, my power, I couldn't. But I vividly recall the moment when the Holy Spirit seemed to envelop me, pulled me up off the floor, and gave me peace that defied my ability to understand it. Now, I'm not saying that I didn't have to walk through this situation and work through my grief because I did, but I had the Holy Spirit, the Helper (the Paraclete, the Intercessor or Advocate) comforting me, lifting me up, and giving me His peace. I don't know if I would've made it without this, but God gave me His peace through my relationship with the Holy Spirit.

You can have all hell breaking loose around you, and you can walk in peace despite the storm.

Longsuffering is a long word that means patience. It endures suffering a long time; it's consistent, steadfast, and perseveres.

Goodness is our ability to give good back instead of evil. It recognizes our true Source, where every good gift comes from, and knowing that we can give out of an endless supply of goodness we tap into through Jesus.

Faithfulness is our ability to stand and keep on standing when everything else is shifting sand. It's our loyalty, our perseverance to stand with others, even when they don't seem to deserve it.

Gentleness is what lets us turn the other cheek; it's uprightness of love and life, virtue. It's what makes us give a kind response that turns away wrath. It isn't weakness; it's strength under control, mildness, and humility.

Self-control is temperance; it's making the right decision and showing restraint, going with what is wise and godly instead of the whims of our flesh.

Each of these things is an element of God's character, and we take on these aspects of His personality as we spend time with the Spirit and follow His leading to Christ and the Father.

If you ask me to show you a Spirit-filled person, I will not point you toward the individual who's manifesting the greatest most obvious gifts. I will point you to the person who is living a lifestyle of this fruit and display them in their lives daily.

Gifts of the Spirit

Anyone who is saved can function in what are called the power gifts—these are the gifts of the Spirit that God uses to empower the believer. As I said earlier, from the time we are saved, the Holy Spirit can rest upon us and manifest these gifts; but these shouldn't be what impress us or what we seek. Fruit is the ongoing evidence of a relationship with the Person of the Holy Spirit.

God gives us the gifts of the Spirit to empower us to do His work (not just for our personal benefit), so while we pray and believe God for compelling works upon the earth, operating in these gifts isn't what shows the depth of our relationship with God. A gift operating in your life isn't what shows your maturity with Christ.

So, yes, we do pray for miraculous signs and wonders; we pray that God will divert storms, give us words of wisdom or knowledge, or heal our loved ones. But the very problems we're praying about are what bring out the fruit of the Spirit in us.

You won't know you have patience until you're stuck in a frustrating circumstance or someones on your nerves. You might pray for God to deliver you from that circumstance, but it's in the middle of it that He can show His evidence in your life. How will you know you know you're long suffering until you've suffered a long time? How will you know you have joy unless you've got the opportunity to despair?

The results of going through trials and the storms of life will reveal your relationship with the Holy Spirit. God can give us spiritual gifts any time; we show maturity and depth of relationship only as we pass through trials and show His character traits in operation in our lives.

Gifts do not build character. Fruit builds our firm foundation in Christ.

The gifts of the Spirit are given to equip us for God's service. We read about them as Paul explains to the Corinthian church:

But the manifestation of the Spirit is given to each one for the profit of all: for to one is given the word of wisdom through the Spirit, to another the word of knowledge through the same Spirit, to another faith by the same Spirit, to another gifts of healings by the same Spirit, to another the working of miracles, to another prophecy, to another discerning of spirits, to another different kinds of tongues, to another the interpretation of tongues.

(1 Corinthians 12: 7-10)

Paul clearly tells us that we receive spiritual gifts so we can help one another—that's important to understand, because if we have the wrong attitude we can think that these gifts are primarily for our personal benefit. Let's take a moment to look at the gifts Paul describes just like we did the fruit.

A word of wisdom is where the Holy Spirit reveals the future prophetically under the anointing of God. A word of knowledge is God revealing information supernaturally that we do not know naturally. The difference between the word of knowledge and the word of wisdom is that the word of knowledge is the revelation of a fact that exists, and the word of wisdom is a revelation of the future. This is what lets us minister to people by telling them things about their lives, like Jesus did to the woman at the well or telling someone what's going to happen in the future, so it points to and gives the glory to God.

The discerning of spirits has to do with comprehending of the human spirit, supernaturally revealed by the Holy Spirit. It is not the discerning of demons, but the discerning of the human spirit—good and bad. People can be manipulative, and we can even fool ourselves about what's in our hearts; the discernment of spirits cuts to the core of the matter and reveals the truth.

The gift of faith is God's bringing to pass a supernatural change. No human effort is involved. We have to have faith that God can do what He says He will do.

The working of miracles is arguably the flashiest; it's where God works a miracle through a human instrument, where a person does a supernatural act by the power of the Holy Spirit. We love to see these, and we pray and ask God for them, but again, remember that we grow and show our maturity when we walk out trials, not when they're diverted my a miracle.

The gift of healing is God supernaturally healing the sick through a ministry or person anointed by the Holy Spirit. A person may be given a gift by the Holy Spirit of God to pray for a particular kind of sickness or disease, and it may only be for a period. This is why there are ministers who operate in this gift frequently, but it's also why a parent can pray with faith over a sick child and expect that God can heal them.

The gift of tongues is the ministry of proclaiming in a public meeting a message from God in a language not understood by the person giving it. It doesn't come from his mind but his spirit, and it isn't the same as a prayer language in tongues. The gift of interpretation operates together with the gift of tongues because when a message is delivered to a body in tongues, to edify those gathered, it must be interpreted. The Holy Spirit supernaturally explains the message in tongues, and in this way, the message given in tongues can bless those who hear it.

Finally, the gift of prophecy is the anointed speaking forth of words of edification, exhortation, and comfort—they're words supernaturally given to the church by God to bless us and lift us up.

Paul frames these gifts up—and those who operate in them—as being like the parts of a body. Each has a purpose, and each is important. Each must act in cooperation with the others. He spends the next few chapters, 1 Corinthians 12, 13, and 14, describing the proper operation of these gifts, and I strongly suggest that you make this part of your personal study.

Particularly important is that Paul puts all gifts into the context of love. He explains that these things are important, but in essence, he returns to what we've been talking about all along—that gifts without relationship (love) are hollow.

Other Roles of the Spirit

Your access to the dunamis power of God is based on your relationship with Him through His Son Jesus by the power of the Holy Spirit. But giving gifts and even filling our lives with fruit are only a few of the roles the Holy Spirit plays in our lives.

One of the greatest parts the Spirit plays in the life of the believer is that of Teacher. Jesus tells us, "But the Helper, the Holy Spirit, whom the Father will send in My name, He will teach you all things, and bring to your remembrance all things that I said to you" (John 14:26). Elsewhere Jesus says, "Now when they bring you to the synagogues and magistrates and authorities, do not worry about how or what you should answer, or what you should say. For the Holy Spirit will teach you in that very hour what you ought to say" (Luke 12:11-12).

When you have a relationship with the Holy Spirit, you have constant access to His teaching. But unlike a human teacher, He teaches us the things of God—in fact, He's the only one who can teach us these things because it takes the Spirit's words to explain spiritual truths (see 1 Corinthians 2:12-16).

Paul explains this when he tells the Corinthians that people without the Holy Spirit find the things of God to be foolishness. He rhetorically asks who can know the Lord's thoughts, and he answers himself by explaining that "we understand these things, for we have the mind of Christ" (1 Corinthians 2:16 NLT).

By depending on the Holy Spirit, you can have the mind of Christ.

One of the Holy Spirit's most well-known names is the Comforter or Counselor. Jesus gives Him this title, which we read in John 14:16—the Paraclete. This is from the word parakletos, which means one called alongside to help. When we speak of the Holy Spirit's role, it is that of a nurturer who cares for us, meeting our needs in a nearly maternal way.

The Holy Spirit's role as Comforter directly opposes the condemnation of the enemy. The Holy Spirit convicts; He does not condemn. Speaking of the Holy Spirit, Jesus says, "And when He has come, He will convict the world of sin, and of righteousness, and of judgment" (John 16:8).

Many have trouble with the distinction, but let me give you a quick primer on the difference between conviction and condemnation. Condemnation tells you that you're a bad person for what you've done. It cuts you down, slashing at your worth and value. In contrast, conviction leads to godly remorse and repentance. Conviction prompts us to turn away from our sin. It doesn't say that we are bad, but it does point out when our actions are ungodly. Conviction doesn't leave us there, however; it prompts us to turn to God in repentance so we can be made right (see 2 Corinthians 7:9-10).

Paul writes, "There is therefore now no condemnation to those who are in Christ Jesus, who do not walk according to the flesh, but according to the Spirit" (Romans 8:1). Guilt and condemnation form a pit that the enemy wants to keep you in so your destiny will go unfulfilled.

Instead of running from the Spirit when we mess up, we should run to Him! The Holy Spirit is the one who will lift us up out of the defeat we fall into and put us back on the path of righteousness. He frees us from the pit and the miry clay, for "the Lord is the Spirit; and where the Spirit of the Lord is, there is liberty" (2 Corinthians 3:17).

In all these things, the Holy Spirit is our Helper. Perhaps none of the ways He helps are as telling as the fact that in addition to being the Convictor of sin, not the condemner, He is also the Intercessor, who opposes the accuser of the brethren.

Paul writes, "Likewise the Spirit also helps in our weaknesses. For we do not know what we should pray for as we ought, but the Spirit Himself makes intercession for us with groanings which cannot be uttered" (Romans 8:26).

These "groanings" are the unutterable gushings of the heart— the overflow of heartfelt emotion that one can only have with someone you're intimately familiar. Why do you want an intimate relationship with the Person of the Holy Spirit? So that He can pour out His heart for you in intercession!

These groanings have been linked to prayer in your spiritual language—in tongues. When we don't know what to pray, we can let the Holy Spirit give utterance for us, with us cooperating by opening our mouths and allowing our prayer language to give voice to the Holy Spirit's prayer for you.

God offers us a prayer language, wherein tongues we communicate secret things to God that the Spirit speaks, and the Father understands (see 1 Corinthians 14:2). Paul says, "For if I pray in tongues, my spirit is praying, but I don't understand what I am saying" (1 Corinthians 14:14 NLT). It bypasses our understanding—it's like a direct line from our spirit, through the Holy Spirit, straight to God.

I want to let you in on a secret: most of my private prayer life is prayer in the Spirit (see Ephesians 6:18). Why? Because I don't always know what I should pray for, and I trust that the Holy Spirit is my Intercessor who will speak through me—though I don't know what I'm saying—the things that He knows I need to pray about. So, like Paul, I pray with words I understand, and I pray a lot in tongues (see 1 Corinthians 14:15)!

I trust what the Spirit wishes to pray for me more than I trust what I want to pray for me! His imagination is limitless, because He is "able, through his mighty power at work within us, to accomplish infinitely more than we might ask or think" (Ephesians 3:20 NLT).

You can probably agree that He knows better than we do. He does not shrink down to the size of our conceptions; He draws us up to think big with Him! Only God's limitless imagination would tell a one-hundred-year-old Abraham that he's going to a mighty nation and have descendants as numerous as the stars! Only God would come up with parting the Red Sea and the Jordan River, of bringing walls down as His people shouted praise to Him, or of raising the dead and making the blind see. Only God would have the idea to put Jesus into the womb of a young virgin and then see Him triumph over hell and the grave, not by fighting a war but by dying on a cross!

His wisdom is foolishness to this world—and that's exactly why the devil can't understand Him and can't do a thing about it! God's vision for you has no limits, so why should you put them on yourself? Let the Holy Spirit pray for you, and then embrace whatever He tells you to do!

You see, the Holy Spirit is our Advisor, and when He gives us direction for our lives, we must listen and obey. He will inform you of wrong decisions before you make them! If we present our ways to the Lord, He will make our paths straight.

He'll explain spiritual truths as we are ready—on His timing, not ours. He does not come to bless our agenda; He reveals the Father's. He doesn't wait for our permission to act; He waits for our surrender.

The Holy Spirit does not move because we want Him to. Instead, He moves when we surrender to Him and thank God for His blessings. We do not command Him; we are grateful to Him for what He's doing. God's character demonstrated in the Word shows us what He's like, and we thank Him for doing in our lives what He's shown He does in the lives of His children—including miracles He works through the power of the Holy Spirit who lives within us.

There's so much more I would like to teach you about the Holy Spirit, but there's just not room in this book for the entirety of His ministry to believers. I wish I had time to get into how He bears witness to Jesus, imparts power to us, works miracles, makes us free from sin and death, and conveys God's love. But you'll have to read about that in a different book if God has me write it!

What I do want to leave you with is the way God poured out the Holy Spirit on the believers gathered on the Day of Pentecost. He did so suddenly on a body of prepared believers, and I believe there are lessons we can take for our spiritual lives from how God poured out His Spirit upon them.

Chapter 17

Are You Ready
for "Suddenly"?

As we've talked about the Holy Spirit, we have spoken about our relationship with the Him as a Person, rather than chasing His moves as though He's a force. This has been so important as a foundation because I often meet people who are either afraid of the Holy Spirit because they've received incorrect teaching or who are chasing after signs, wonders, and power at the expense of actually knowing Him.

However, this is only part of it. Yes, our personal relationship with the Spirit is incredibly important, and it's the foundation in our lives. But when we read the account of the Day of Pentecost in Acts, we do not see the Spirit falling on individual believers as they went about their private lives; He fell in a corporate setting while they were all gathered together.

So while we know the Holy Spirit intimately and personally, His operation in our lives is generally for our benefit as a Body— the Body of Christ—and for the world God wants to save.

In One Accord

Let's return to one of the Scriptures we used to start this study of Pentecost, Acts 2:1-4, and pull something more from it:

When the Day of Pentecost had fully come, they were all with one accord in one place. And suddenly there came a sound from heaven, as of a rushing mighty wind, and it filled the whole house where they were sitting. Then there appeared to them divided tongues, as of fire, and one sat upon each of them. And they were all filled with the Holy Spirit and began to speak with other tongues, as the Spirit gave them utterance.

I want to draw your attention to some different parts of this verse. The first is that they were gathered together "with one accord."

This word we translate accord is a unique Greek word that's used only used a handful of times in the New Testament, and almost all of them are in Acts. The word means in harmony— it's in one mind, with one accord, with one person, and it's a compound of two root words we'd translate as "rush along" and "in unison."

I love the imagery there: rushing along toward God together in harmony and unity. I hope you grasp this: our depth with the Holy Spirit grows in the intimate personal relationship, but the believers of the Early Church received Him as they rushed toward God together with one accord!

If you are trying to do this Christian life by yourself, thinking all that matters is just you and Jesus, you are robbing yourself of something amazing.

Something powerful happens when we walk in agreement.

We need one another. We need each other's support, encouragement, prayers, admonition, and wisdom. These founders of the Early Church were not secluded away, each seeking God in his or her own way; they were praying together, seeking Him as one body.

I want to return to Paul's description of the spiritual gifts from 1 Corinthians 12 that we talked about earlier, because after he had explained how the gifts operate in the Church, he used the example of a human body to help us understand that they all function together. Paul writes,

> For as the body is one and has many members, but all the members of that one body, being many, are one body, so also is Christ. For by one Spirit we were all baptized into one body—whether Jews or Greeks, whether slaves or free—and have all been made to drink into one Spirit. For in fact, the body is not one member but many.
> (1 Corinthians 12-12-13)

We as Christians—or as members of a congregation—are all part of the Body of Christ. We're not lone soldiers, fighting against sin, just us and Jesus. We're part of something bigger that God empowers by His Holy Spirit so that the whole world can come to know His Son.

Paul goes on to explain that we can't simply decide that we don't want to be part of the Body of Christ because our function—our gift—isn't what we wish it were. Nor can everyone be like us, with the same gift. We all have different gifts, and we all need each other! Paul finishes, "But our bodies have many parts, and God has put each part just where he wants it" (1 Corinthians 12:18 NLT).

So what part are you? Are you a hand? A foot? An eye? If you've never studied your spiritual gifts, I suggest you hop online and look for a spiritual gift test and begin to learn about the gifts that God has put into you, because you have something to offer the Body of Christ. And we need it!

God Has a "Suddenly" for You

The final part of Pentecost I want to look at is how God did the pouring when He poured out His Spirit. If you back up in Acts, before the Day of Pentecost, you'll remember that Jesus told them to go and wait for the promise—the outpouring of God's Spirit (see Acts 1:4-5).

After Jesus had ascended into Heaven, they returned to Jerusalem and went upstairs into the upper room—possibly the same upper room where they'd had the Lord's Supper before Jesus was crucified. Luke, the writer of Acts, tells us about the disciples who were there, and then he writes this: "These all continued with one accord in prayer and supplication, with the women and Mary the mother of Jesus, and with His brothers" (Acts 1:14). We learn there were about 120 of them there, and they were preparing to receive what Jesus had promised by being in one accord (there's that word again) in prayer.

They were still there meeting when the Day of Pentecost fully came—and then, suddenly, something happened.

They spent time in prayer and preparation in obedience to Jesus, but when it was time for God to pour out His Spirit, it happened suddenly. The word "suddenly" we read in Acts 2:2 means instantly and has the root meaning of opening the eyes and happening unexpectedly.

Catch this! We prepare; we seek God. But when He falls, He does so quickly and unexpectedly. And I believe that God has four areas of unexpected blessing He'd like you to catch that He showed me in the Word from other times He moved suddenly.

The first is restoration. Many of you reading this are tired, worn out, burned out, depressed, and broken down by cares, disappointments, and bad life events. I believe God wants to restore you, and He gave me the example of King Hezekiah in the Old Testament. When Hezekiah realized the people had strayed from God and that they were in despair, he sought God's presence. They offered burnt offerings to the Lord, and we read, "So the service of the house of the Lord was set in order. Then Hezekiah and all the people rejoiced that God had prepared the people, since the events took place so suddenly" (2 Chronicles 29:35b-36).

You may be hurting, burned out, or far from God. But you can turn to Him, and He will restore you suddenly!

The second blessing I feel God wants to give you is a victory over your enemies. David writes, "Let all my enemies be ashamed and greatly troubled; let them turn back and be ashamed suddenly" (Psalms 6:10). Who is our enemy? The devil! He comes to steal, kill, and destroy, but God wants to restore to you what he has stolen—and He wants to do it suddenly!

You may feel trapped right now, but God has sudden deliverance for you, as well. When Paul and Silas were in prison, instead of sulking and having a pity party, they praised and worshiped. And what happened? Suddenly there was an earthquake, their chains broke, and the very foundations of the prison were shaken (see Acts 16:25-32)! God has a "suddenly" for your deliverance!

The last thing God showed me He has done suddenly is revival. In the wake of the Spirit falling on those in the upper room, Peter—the same Peter who denied Jesus three times only weeks before—boldly stepped up to answer the questions and mockery of the crowd. Inspired by the Holy Spirit, Peter preaches to the crowd and proclaims the Lordship of Jesus Christ to the very Jews who'd rejected Him. He explains that the tongues and other manifestations of the Spirit they were seeing were the fulfillment of Joel's prophecy that God would pour out His Spirit upon all flesh.

And what was the result of Peter's message? Revival! "And with many other words he testified and exhorted them, saying, 'Be saved from this perverse generation.' Then those who gladly received his word were baptized; and that day about three thousand souls were added to them" (Acts 2:40-41). Three thousand people were added to the church that day—I'd call that quite a revival!

But it didn't end there. The Spirit inspired them to teach, fellowship, share meals, and pray and a deep sense of awe came over everyone as the apostles performed miraculous signs and wonders (see Acts 2:42-43).

These people were the same Jews who'd crucified Christ. But when the Spirit fell, revival suddenly sprang up, and it forever changed the baby Church that had just been born.

God has a "suddenly" move of His Spirit for you. You may have been preparing for it for years, or you may just have been saved. When God pours out His Spirit, it will change your world suddenly! I pray you're able to receive the restoration, the victory over your enemy, the deliverance, and the revival that God has for you. He delivers it through His Holy Spirit, and He will do so when you're in one accord with the believers around you.

God has set divine appointments throughout history, and He has one with you, dear friend—a date for a sudden outpouring of His Holy Spirit!

Chapter 18

Obedience Is Your Key

I have so enjoyed diving deeper into the principles behind the biblical feasts with you! I am passionate about getting to know our Lord better and helping others do so, and I hope and pray that you've been able to draw closer to God by seeing His character demonstrated through these feasts.

Some detractors may argue that the promises God gave His people in these feasts were for them then, not us now. But I believe that He is the same yesterday, today, and forever and that He changes not. And because we serve a God in whom there is no shadow of turning, I feel that we can apply the principles behind these promises to our lives today!

Throughout history, God has made appointments to bless His people. These special days weren't for His benefit; they were for ours. They were opportunities to remember Him, focus on Him, and draw near to Him. And while we don't celebrate them the same way the Children of Israel did, I can't imagine a better way of loving on my Lord and Savior than by stopping and taking the time to remember, focus, and draw near to Him!

God has divine appointments He wants to set with you, dear reader. He wants to make days and times special, and He yearns to show you His blessings just as He desired to bless the Children of Israel.

But He has given us a choice. We can choose to obey Him, to learn from the eternal principles He established in His Word, and to let these things impact our hearts...

...Or we can let our hearts be hard and miss precious opportunities to meet with Him.

I don't know about you, but I don't want to miss even a single opportunity to draw near to the One who loved me and called me out of the darkness and into the light!

You've now seen some of the ways God blessed His people through the feasts He instituted, and now it is your job to let this knowledge become understanding and let understanding birth movement. It's your job to let Him position you and prepare your heart by being soft, moldable, and willing to follow the principles He's outlined in His Word.

Your obedience is your key—it will open the path to untold blessings from the Lord. He is not waiting up in Heaven to create blessings; He's already done so, and you must only appropriate them!

Jesus fulfilled every single prophecy and expectation that God laid out in the Old Testament, and He was the ultimate fulfillment and sacrifice in every possible way. He has done it all on the cross, and He has grafted us into the same promises and blessings that God established for His people, the Jews. We are now Abraham's spiritual descendants, and we are now co-heirs with Christ Jesus of eternal blessings.

He paid for it all. It is finished. There's nothing left to be done...

...except receive.

So will you? Will you draw near and let God's love change you, bless you, and empower you? I certainly hope so!

There is a great harvest of souls the Lord wants to equip us to bring in, and every principle, blessing, and gift He has to offer are for one purpose and one purpose alone—to make His name great on the earth so that none should perish but all find eternal life.

Now, accept His empowerment and get out there to do the good work He has destined you to do!